Nine Lives

WALDEMAR LOTNIK was born in 1925 near Lublin, where he was brought up on his grandfather's farm until he was seven. His parents then fetched him to live in Kremenets, a garrison town in the Polish part of the Ukraine. After the events described in this book, he settled in London where he still lives. He is married with two children and four grandchildren and has not been back to Poland since he left in the summer of 1945.

JULIAN PREECE was born in Birmingham in 1962 and brought up in Somerset. He studied German and French at Oxford and now teaches German and Comparative Literature at the University of Kent at Canterbury. His *Günter Grass and the Germans: Literature, History, Politics* is forthcoming.

NINE LIVES

Ethnic Conflict in the Polish-Ukrainian Borderlands

Waldemar Lotnik
with
Julian Preece

Foreword by Neal Ascherson

Serif
London

First published 1999 by
Serif
47 Strahan Road
London E3 5DA

British Library Cataloguing-in-Publication Data.
A catalogue record for this book is available from the British Library.

Library of Congress Cataloging-in-Publication Data.
A catalog record for this book is available from the Library of Congress.

ISBN 1 897959 40 0

This book is dedicated to the memory of those men and
women who gave their lives for the cause of Polish
freedom in the Second World War.

Typeset in North Wales by Derek Doyle and Associates,
Mold, Flintshire
Printed and bound in Ireland by
ColourBooks Ltd, Dublin

Contents

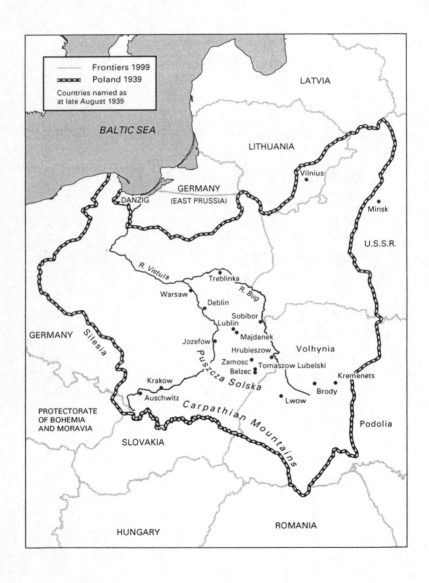

Foreword

This is one of the most tragic and horrifying memoirs to emerge from the Second World War. At its centre is an episode so dreadful – and so firmly suppressed by the Communist authorities of Poland and the Soviet Union – that it has taken 50 years for a candid account to appear in English. This is the genocidal war fought between Ukrainian and Polish partisans in the borderlands either side of the River Bug, a merciless war of mutual extermination which cost tens of thousands of lives – almost all civilians – and which was routinely accompanied by massacre, rape and torture on a Rwandan or Bosnian scale.

Waldemar Lotnik was sucked into this bloodbath as a teenager. He fought as a Polish guerrilla against the Ukrainian bands, who were closely supported by the Nazi Wehrmacht. Half a century on, he has the courage to admit and describe his own share in the killings of prisoners and civilians, and the far worse atrocities committed by some of his own comrades. History will judge whether the Ukrainians behaved with even greater savagery, as Lotnik claims.

Because of the author's fearless candour, *Nine Lives* is a unique witness to the terrifying moral and political chaos which fell on Poland as the war ended and Soviet troops replaced the Nazis. He was put into the Nazi death camp of Majdanek, which he only just survived. Emaciated but free, he was recruited into the new Communist armed forces of Poland and sent to Russia to train as a Soviet intelligence agent. Defecting, he joined the remnant of Poland's non-Communist partisan army now fighting a hopeless guerrilla war against the Soviet occupation.

Finally, he decided to escape and, after many incredible adventures and brushes with death, reached the American zone of Germany.

This is an unforgettable book. Lotnik's story is not comfortable reading, but it is essential: a missing fragment of the history of this barbarous continent.

Neal Ascherson

1

Caught in the Middle

On making out the sound of engines, a German armoured column rumbling its way to the River Bug, we waited, spell-bound, until the tanks loomed into sight. I dived for cover, sure that they would start shooting.

'They're not interested in you, you ninny!' my aunt shouted with a confidence which hardly seemed appropriate. But she was right and we went home that evening as though we had seen nothing unusual. It was not until the next day that we heard the heavy, regular thud of artillery, repulsed on this occasion by the Poles.

War had been on everyone's lips all through the summer of '39, but no one had an inkling of what war would turn out to mean. Because I would do anything to avoid sitting in lessons, the prospect sounded exciting. It tasted of adventure and escape, while the uncertainty did not make me feel afraid. Towards the end of August my mother telephoned my father at his army base in Kremenets, perched close to the border with the Soviet Union deep in the Polish part of the Ukraine, and asked if we should risk returning. Under no circumstances, came the reply: the base had been put on red alert.

In the year before the secret pact between Poland's two mighty neighbours, Hitler's Germany and Stalin's Russia, ended Poland's brief interlude of independence, collections for national defence at school had heralded the impending conflict. Jewish boys gave enormous sums: they knew what was already happening in Germany. My mother handed me ten zlotys, by any reckoning a large amount of money, and when I asked her why the Jewish boys had donated far more, she just said that in times of adversity we faced common enemies and had no choice but to stick together. As the danger increased by the day, it was Hitler rather than Stalin we feared, even though the Soviets sat right on our doorstep.

Two and a half weeks after the German invasion, the Soviets crossed Poland's eastern border on 17 September, ready to claim the spoils they had been promised. The Polish army proved easy prey. Demoralised by failure elsewhere, co-ordinated resistance all but ceased once the enemy had advanced much more than 30 miles. Only independent battalions continued the fight, but the Soviets still suffered casualties running into tens of thousands before their share of Polish territory became incorporated into the Union of Soviet Socialist Republics. My father's unit in far-away Kremenets surrendered after enemy tanks had encircled the garrison town. While most of his comrades were marched into captivity, he escaped, hiding with Polish families until the invaders had moved further west. As an officer who had served in Pilsudski's legions, they would doubtless have shot him at Katyn had he not slipped away.

Our attitude was fatalistic, self-preservation our priority, but in fact we suffered no untoward hardship over the next few months. The real terror, finally unleashed after Germany turned on Russia in 1941, began slowly for most civilian, non-Jewish Poles. Uncertainty proved to be our principal foe, a demon which gnawed at us and refused to go away. What was happening to my father? Where were my uncles, Kasimir, Joseph, Anthony and Stanislaw? Had my schoolfriends back in Kremenets found safety?

Uncle Stanislaw, the most dissolute of my mother's five brothers, was also trapped in the Soviet zone. We did not see either him or my father until late in the autumn, by which time Poland was well and truly beaten, the Germans there to stay and the Soviets entrenched east of the River Bug. My father's main fear had apparently not been death but that he would end up with a red star rather than a cross over his grave. My cousin Peter, a would-be flying ace who had given me a spin in his machine two summers previously, was the only member of the family to escape abroad and fight with the Free Poles. He flew his plane to Hungary in the hope of reaching France or England, but the Hungarians confiscated it and made him carry on under his own steam. A year later he was flying Spitfires in the Battle of Britain before ending up in a German POW camp. Those of us who stayed behind had a harder time of it.

Hrubieszow, the nearest town to my maternal grandfather's farm, which stood between the Ukrainian village of Modryn and its twin Polish settlement of Modryniec and where I had spent the first seven years of my life with my grandparents and five uncles, did not fall without a fight, however. In Modryn itself the whole village watched a Soviet cavalry unit gallop in formation across the crest of a hill only to flee in panic when two Poles, positioned on a narrow bridge with a machine gun, took them by surprise and sprayed them with fire. Just two soldiers and one gun! If that was all the mighty Red Army was capable of, then we reckoned that against the Soviets alone we could have more than held our own, as had happened when they invaded under Trotsky in the Russo-Polish War of 1919–21. But two days later the Russians returned in greater numbers and captured the two soldiers.

As far as fighting was concerned that, for the time being, was that. Hrubieszow, on the western bank of the Bug 150 miles south-east of Lublin, lay directly on the new border between the Soviet and German zones of occupation and there was confusion over which pieces of territory had been handed to whom. We were invaded first by the Germans, then occupied by the Soviets and finally handed back again to the Germans, all within the space of a fortnight.

The Soviets made a ramshackle army. While they had far more heavy equipment than the Poles, their strength, as throughout Russian history, lay in sheer numbers rather than discipline or equipment. Recruited from the vast peasantry, their soldiers had been born into hardship. They could survive two or three weeks in the field with the rations they carried with them, mainly large quantities of unpalatable black bread. While each possessed his own wooden spoon and container for collecting rations of gruel, they had no change of clothes in their knapsacks. Instead of socks they wrapped long, filthy rags around their feet, which made their whole bodies stink of cheap industrial boot polish.

One of the dozen Soviet soldiers billeted at our farm held hushed conversations with my grandfather. He confided that most of his family had perished in the famines of the 1930s during Stalin's notorious 'reorganisation of the countryside'. This man had volunteered for that most pressing reason of self-interest: survival. He seemed much older than the others, who were mainly fresh-faced boys, and as we had language and much else in common, it was not always easy to see him, or indeed the others, as an enemy.

All my ancestors come from the eastern part of Poland annexed by the Russians after the great partition at the end of the eighteenth century, when Prussia, Austria and Russia chopped up Poland to share it out among themselves. Before the First World War my grandfather had served in the Imperial Guard in Saint Petersburg. On his bedroom wall hung a large portrait of Nicolas II flanked by his personal Cossacks. My grandfather stood in his sumptuous uniform in the second row, staring intently at the camera.

Most of my family had always spoken Russian, some fluently, and had been educated in Russian, though like most Poles they resented Russian rule and preferred to speak Polish among themselves. If they had gone to school, they also knew German. As a boy I learnt three languages in addition to my native Polish: Ukrainian, which I learnt at school, as well as Russian and Byelorussian. I was taught two alphabets, the Roman (for Polish) and the Cyrillic (for Russian), and knew the rituals of the Catholics, the Russian Orthodox and the Catholic Orthodox (or Greek Catholics as we called them), as well as those of the Jews.

Caught in the Middle

What I knew about the Germans I gained from first-hand experience during summer vacation tours of Poland. My school sent us on trips to visit Poland's historic sites, taking us through German settlements, mainly in the west, which always appeared far superior to the Polish, Ukrainian or Czech settlements through which we passed. In Krakow we filed past the embalmed bodies of the Polish kings and listened to the horn-blower at St Mary's Church, who still sounded his horn four times an hour, facing towards each point of the compass in turn. The original horn-blower in the Middle Ages had warned the people of advancing Mongol armies. An arrow had pierced his neck as he gave his third blast.

It was not until I was seven that I was taken from my grand-parents' farm to join my parents in Kremenets, just three miles from Bolshevik Russia. These are Ukrainian territories, rolling plains of wheat, marshland and woods broken up by hilly out-crops, which belonged to Poland between the two world wars after the Polish national hero, Marshal Pilsudski, had pushed back the frontiers in 1920. He had seized his moment when the military giants of Russia and Germany both lay exhausted and captured land which the Soviets did not take back until 1945. Perhaps he thereby sowed the seeds of the future Polish-Ukrainian tragedy, as he succeeded while the Ukrainians under Petlura failed. The short-lived Free Ukraine was choked in the revolutionary battles between the Reds and the Whites, then crushed by Trotsky's armies, as most of the Ukraine was turned into a Soviet republic. Instead of helping his Ukrainian neigh-bours, Pilsudski had invaded on his march to Russia, reaching as far as Kiev and alienating his supposed Ukrainian allies. The Bolsheviks then drove the Poles back to the banks of the Vistula on the very edge of Warsaw, but Pilsudski's outnumbered legions repulsed them and recaptured large tracts of the western Ukraine, which were subsequently incorporated into the new, resurrected post-war Polish state.

The new Polish-Soviet border ran right through the Ukraine and demarcated a national and political boundary, the Iron Curtain of the inter-war years, separating the old from the new order, agrarian capitalism with its peasant smallholdings and seigneurial estates from the emerging world of communism and collectivisation. As a result the Bolsheviks were the bogeymen of my childhood. My teachers in Kremenets cast them in the role of the Mongol invaders who had swept through Poland many centuries before. If I was angry with my little brother or with a playmate at school, there was nothing meaner to call him than 'a dirty Bolshevik'.

In the eyes of the local Ukrainian peasants, the Poles were the new colonisers. They regarded us as successors to the pre-war Tsarists and believed we had collaborated with the foreign occupiers during partition. For the first few years the Polish military struggled to put down marauding units of guerrillas and saboteurs. It was because of that danger and the general insecurity that my parents had originally left me with my mother's family when my father was sent to his new posting. But it was with Ukrainians that I spent most of my childhood, learnt to read and write, skated on frozen lakes in winter and discovered shards of Russian and German ammunition, left over from the First World War, in the forests and fields round about Kremenets. We collected this debris with a passion, searched for it in the undergrowth, swapped treasured pieces with each other, sometimes discovering unexploded shells and even hand-grenades. We could tell at a glance what had come from which side, so great was our interest in weapons and soldiers. At the age of eight I had learnt the names and types of all the rifles, cannons and other military paraphernalia; at twelve I could throw a hand-grenade and dismantle a rifle blindfold, just as the new recruits were trained to do at the base.

Poles treated the locals with a suspicious respect, which was not always unwarranted. No Ukrainians, for instance, were permitted to work in government service, not even as train drivers or minor officials, for fear they would form a fifth column in the event of an invasion. Even our family maid was forced to return home every evening from the base. But the Ukrainian language and Ukrainian history were taught in schools, alongside the Polish language and Polish history. There was freedom in matters of religion. The Orthodox and the Catholics mixed easily, although the difference between Poles and Ukrainians was primarily religious, rather than linguistic or ethnic: if an Orthodox Ukrainian converted to Roman Catholicism then he automatically became Polish and vice versa. Across the border, where the large majority of Ukrainians lived, they suffered some of the worst of Stalin's excesses: their churches were torched, their clergy and intelligentsia deported to Siberia and their land collectivised. They counted their dead in millions. The Ukrainians in Volhynia still resented Polish rule, however.

My initial excitement at the prospect of war had begun to ebb after I had seen the two Polish soldiers captured at Modryn and after two of my uncles, the fearless Anthony and Jack-the-lad Kasimir, who had been involved in the fighting on the River Bug, returned home in late October. They had ditched their uniforms and fled on foot, and their dejection now infected the mood at the farm. Anthony had been eager join up, convinced he would be back by the New Year with a clutch of medals and a glorious war record. Only heroes would prosper in a victorious post-war Poland, he reasoned. Like his brothers, he was indeed home by Christmas, safe and sound for the moment, but footsore and bedraggled rather than bathed in glory. Three of my uncles, Anthony, Kasimir and Joseph, the smallest of the five and perhaps for that reason the most hot-headed, drifted towards the partisans. The other two, Stanislaw, who knew how to keep out of trouble, and Edek, the youngest, who was sent to work in a German factory, would be the only two to survive the war.

Other Polish soldiers arrived on our doorstep through the autumn. They dumped their weapons – bayonets, rifles and pistols – for my grandfather to bury in case of German searches, and continued their journey home after a night's rest. Because the Polish army disbanded in this way and because later, once the fighting began in earnest on the Eastern Front and abandoned Soviet equipment became plentiful, the Polish Resistance never suffered from a severe shortage of arms. Butter, to paraphrase Goebbels, might have been in short supply, but not guns.

At the beginning of the war the Germans recruited workers for their factories as volunteers rather than deported them as slaves. They paid them too, not as much as a German worker but enough to send something home. Many Ukrainians volunteered at first, as well as some of the poorer Poles. A young man from a neighbouring village told me that he had never lived better than when working on a farm in Germany. He was permitted to return home once a year for a holiday, could write letters to relatives and after work was allowed to travel freely or go to the cinema. Home on leave, he might even be saluted by a German soldier checking his papers.

For the Ukrainians, the German presence signified change in a different sense. Initially, in that brief period in mid-September 1939, they had been tempted to help the Soviets, thinking, as disgruntled peoples down the ages have always thought, that their enemy's enemy was their friend. I had recognised some who thought it their duty to round up defeated Polish soldiers and hand them over to the Soviets, but the welcome they extended to the Germans was much more jubilant. They brought them bread and salt, according to a time-honoured greeting. In return the Germans replaced minor Polish officials with Ukrainians whenever possible. A village church, which in 1921 had been 'polonised', that is converted from the Orthodox to the Catholic faith, was handed back to the Ukrainians. Near Hrubieszow Poles and Ukrainians had lived in mixed communities for centuries: Polish villages bordered on Ukrainian villages and rivalry had rarely given cause for violence. Now suddenly the Ukrainian settlements became enemy territory and Polish villages our safe havens. The Ukrainian priest in Modryn angered my grandparents by inviting the Germans to graze their cart-horses in our fields, claiming they were his own. When my grandfather stopped him in the street, he announced that all Polish land in Modryn now belonged to his people. Yet this was an incongruous alliance, for the Master Race could barely disguise its contempt for the uncouth Ukrainian peasantry.

Of more use to the Germans than the Ukrainians were the

so-called *Volksdeutsche*, descendants of German settlers from past centuries (some of whom had arrived as long as six hundred years ago, only a little later than the Jews), whose farmsteads punctuated the plains of Eastern Europe. They sometimes spoke only rudimentary German but had retained their German names and a vestigial sense of their German origins. Many now flocked to serve their supposed liberators from the far-away Fatherland, who gave them Polish land and property and allotted them posts and responsibilities stripped from Poles. There were also Poles who claimed German ancestry in order to get hold of a German passport and the double or treble ration coupons, the good jobs, privileges and even houses which went with it. We hated them even more than we hated the Germans and the partisans exacted ruthless revenge when they got hold of them. Two such Poles I knew claimed *volksdeutsch* status in order to act as double agents and pass on information to the Resistance.

At the beginning of the Occupation, in fact up to some time in 1942, the Germans made Polish farms provide so many tons of grain, gallons of milk or head of cattle, which they transported back to the Reich or used to feed their soldiers. All livestock had to be registered, marked with a clip attached to the ear of each animal, and permission was needed in order to slaughter even a single pig. Failure to comply could result in summary execution. Within a year the Germans doubled the production quotas, which had to be handed over in exchange for ration coupons, soon to become far more valuable than the old Polish currency. A Polish-speaking official came to live on the estate owned by my father's father in Zakzrouvek, a village to the west of Zamosc, to supervise the provision of these goods. He was tongue-tied and aloof and we thought of him as a spy, even though he remained perfectly civil. At Zakzrouvek, where we had lakes chock-full of carp, a mill and a spanking new hydro-electric dam, we never managed more than a fifth of what they wanted – even a mechanised farm could not have produced goods and crops in such quantities. Yet no matter what the Germans took, they gave us a stamped receipt, as if the theft had been a business transaction and we had been paid rather than robbed. After 1942 this pretence ceased and they simply confiscated what they wanted.

I passed my school leaving certificate in the summer of 1941, two months before my sixteenth birthday, in the same week that the German armies rolled east. Yet even after the invasion of Russia in June 1941 school did not cease for me, as I moved to a higher technical college, this time in Hrubieszow itself. I lodged with a beautiful but partially crippled landlady who entertained a Ukrainian lover, the commander of the local militia which by then had taken over local policing duties. It was as if by associating with him that she got her revenge for the disappointments and the slights she must have suffered from Polish men on account of her disability. Now she found herself on the winning side.

At this new college we had lathes and machine tools, learnt how to weld and forge metals, calculate stress levels and measure the effects of temperature changes. When high-quality scrap became available from the Eastern Front, the lecturers set us an industrial task: the construction of two military lorries. The class rose to the challenge with enthusiasm and succeeded in making two workable vehicles – engines, drive shafts, gear boxes and bodywork. Once finished we made no attempt to disguise our pride and even posed to be filmed for the German newsreels, which showed our beaming faces throughout occupied Europe. The commentary lauded our commitment to the German cause and held us up as an example of what Polish students could achieve under German supervision. At that point, some time in the summer of 1942, I decided that continuing with my studies amounted to collaboration and that I could have no more to do with it.

2

Escalation

The first time my family suffered an irredeemable loss was when my Uncle Joseph was shot some time before June 1941. Since from childhood he had been forced to compensate for his size, he was the most fearless of my uncles. Such qualities can be fatal, but I never discovered exactly what happened to him. My surviving uncles and grandparents refused to discuss dangerous subjects in my presence for fear I might blurt out something at the wrong moment. Everyone who knew what happened to Joseph is now dead. I believed for a long time that he had been present with his brother Kasimir at some sort of gathering in Hrubieszow which had involved Germans and Ukrainians – though why as Poles they should have been present I can't say, and the question did not occur to me until I came to piece together this story – and that he had been stupid enough to shout out something to the effect that the Germans would not be in charge forever, or that one day they would be made to pay for their crimes. On reflection, it seems more likely that he and Kasimir had been asked to do something or other for the Germans and, refusing, had insulted the soldiers. Open dissent like that could lead to a quick killing. I know that the body arrived back at our house, that it was identified and that we held a funeral, which makes it highly unlikely that he was executed or died in combat. I do remember that his widow kept fainting at his funeral before trying to jump into the open grave and be buried with him.

Kasimir, who had broken so many girls' hearts before the war, found himself on the run from this moment. He fled to the farm in Modryn, where my grandfather held frantic discussions with him out of my eager earshot. I remember my grandfather getting out his secret 'treasure drawer', which contained gold roubles saved up from long-gone Tsarist times, and saw Kasimir stuff his pockets with money before disappearing. By the time the Gestapo called, he had vanished. 'You killed him,' Grandfather said in response to their questions. Kasimir was to spend two and a half years in the underground, working as a messenger between various Polish units. On the few occasions when he turned up unexpectedly at the farm, he crept into the house after dark. My grandfather died a few months after his last such visit at Christmas 1943 when Kasimir was tortured to death by the Ukrainian militia.

Uncle Stanislaw was not interested in feats of bravery, nor was he the sort of man to cling to principles, which he did not possess anyway, if he might have to pay for them with his life. When the Germans first arrived, they sent him to work in a power station where he quickly picked up a working knowledge of German. By the summer of Joseph's death he had landed a comfortable job in a club for German officers. Here he prospered for a couple of years, organising shifts for the Polish waiting staff while taking advantage of his all-night pass to smuggle out goods to sell on the black market. My other uncles teased him by calling him a collaborator and said that he would apply to be the next Führer.

I had my own first brush with death when I foolishly strayed into the centre of Modryn where a Wehrmacht company was billeted. 'Brush with death' is the wrong expression if taken to mean that I had merely been in some danger of dying: most people experience moments at some time in their lives when death seems a distinct possibility – perhaps for a split second, maybe for a little longer. What I recall was a distinct certainty rather than a possibility – the sure knowledge that in a few seconds I would cease to exist. The condemned man who is granted a reprieve moments before the sentence is due to be carried out knows this feeling and all who have experienced it agree that it concentrates the mind to an absolute degree. I can recall every second of the incident.

I was standing at the far end of the village square watching the German troops outside their HQ as they swigged vodka straight from the bottle. A very drunk Hauptmann suddenly noticed me and shouted at me to step towards him, brandishing a pistol in the air as he got to his feet and laughing at himself and his own bravado. The others watched him. When I reached him, he pointed his pistol at my forehead, repeatedly yelled '*Polnische Schweine*' and started slowly to pull back the trigger. I could see the bullet inside as the drum began to revolve and I knew that these were the last seconds of my life. They lasted an eternity. Then there came a deafening crack followed by a ringing buzz in my left ear and the stench of cordite.

He had thought better of killing me, or maybe all along had just wanted the fun of scaring me, and had fired a fraction of an inch above my head, having jerked the pistol upwards just before pulling the trigger. I was deaf in my left ear for weeks. Many times since then I have been on the point of falling asleep when I have heard that bang and smelt that cordite.

Three Jewish families lived in Modryn. One was an elderly couple who had lived alone after their only son had moved to the city. What befell them, or when it befell them, I don't know. Neither did I notice what happened to the second family and can only remember that they had owned some sort of business, as did the third, who lived, unusually for Jews, in the centre of the Ukrainian village. Their shop sold hardware and domestic utensils, pickled herrings, tobacco and eggs, but I remember them because of their beautiful daughter who swayed gently from side to side as she walked, her right hand held out in an infatuating gesture.

Before the war she had started to see a Polish boy known as Baron, who was said to be related to me distantly – I think our grandmothers were second or third cousins. He was three or four years older than me and had been brought up by his mother on a remote farmstead on the edge of the forest.

People said it was because he had no father that he became a petty thief and a hoodlum, boasting a criminal record by his late teens when the war started. But he was also naturally charming and when he had got a job at the Jewish shop, shifting boxes and serving behind the counter, he fell in love with the daughter and she with him. When her parents discovered their affair, they dismissed him and forbade the pair to see each other again. After that they met secretly in the fields and woods roundabout.

She had been lying with him in the grass one afternoon when her younger brother ran to tell her that their parents had been arrested. From that moment all three took to the forests where Baron had made himself a dug-out, carved from the earth beneath a large oak tree, in which he intended to hide if the police came after him. All three could sleep there comfortably in the summer and autumn and Baron had stored enough supplies to last a few weeks. For a while they lived in relative safety, coming out at night to light a fire at some distance from their hide-out and to cook food, which Baron had usually stolen from Ukrainian peasants, whom he now, like the rest of us, regarded as his enemies. He had begun to rob Ukrainian officials and took watches and money, as well as food. He had a couple of rifles, one or two pistols and even a few hand-grenades that he had picked up from the defeated Polish troops in the autumn of 1939. When his victims resisted, he killed them.

To kill a Ukrainian in pursuit of loot was not high up on the list of crimes for the Germans and they did not bother to pursue him, if indeed they heard of his exploits amidst the general mayhem. They would have thought of Baron as a common criminal rather than a partisan, as he disguised his assassinations as robberies. For me, he was a Robin Hood of the Polish Resistance and I admired his courage and secretly wanted to emulate his deeds. When I finally ran away to join the partisans, it was his example which inspired me.

When his assassinations took on an unmistakably political character, the authorities did begin to take an interest in Baron.

Escalation

His days were numbered after he had killed a particularly unpopular Ukrainian who ran the co-operative dairy. His victim had replaced a mild-mannered Polish official who had attempted to persuade the Germans that their imposed quotas were hopelessly unrealistic. Perhaps because he had been instructed to follow the letter of the law, the Ukrainian replacement did all in his power to harass the Polish farmers into meeting the production targets. Even some of his compatriots took exception to his methods, and after his death their general view seemed to be that he who lives by the sword shall perish by the sword. I felt so intrigued by the murder that I made my way to the church where his body lay. There was nobody to mourn him, as no one knew where he came from, and I remember feeling puzzled that no one had placed a cross on his body, as was the custom. Whether that was a careless oversight or a deliberate omission, it created an awful impression of godlessness which felt entirely appropriate.

Even after this assassination the Germans did not look for Baron straightaway, despite the fact that everyone who lived nearby knew that he had carried out the killing. It was several weeks afterwards that three German SS men arrived in Modryn on a two-horse sleigh, stopping first at the dairy, where they had a drink with the new foreman and asked a few questions, before setting off in the direction of Baron's mother's house, where they drew up at about noon. Baron still visited his mother and younger brother and could hide in the loft above the front door if he felt in danger. His luck must have been running out by this time because he was there when the SS sleigh approached. Two men went into the house and got their business over with quickly. They turned to depart leaving two bodies on the floor, those of Baron's mother and younger brother, both with bullets in their heads. But as they reached the exit, Baron shot them from the loft through the open hatch. He then jumped down as the third SS man made off in the sleigh. Even though Baron wounded him, the German was able to return to Hrubieszow to raise the alarm.

While the killing of a few Ukrainians might pass more or less unnoticed and the assassination of a Ukrainian official not bring the weight of the law down on the killer immediately, to shoot two SS men and wound a third was a different matter and would be avenged ruthlessly. The following day three dozen troops in armoured vehicles rattled into Modryn. Once they had failed to discover Baron, they arrested 60 young Polish men from the surrounding villages. Ukrainian militia based east of the Bug combed the area, stopped and harassed passers-by and enforced the curfew with extra diligence. Meanwhile the SS took the hostages to Hrubieszow for interrogation, which served little purpose since none of them knew Baron's whereabouts any more than their interrogators. What was unusual in this case was that the hostages survived. Once the Germans had found and killed Baron, they released them.

Baron was now well and truly holed up in the forests with his two companions and had to go further and further afield to forage for food. In winter it is always much more difficult to survive than in summer, the dug-out must have been dripping with water, if not covered in icicles, and the depth of the snow would have made lighting a fire an arduous task. Now armed militia posed a constant threat to them. Soon Baron was stopped at night by a patrol and killed a soldier before escaping, lightly wounded, back to his hide-out. He needed medical attention and could no longer venture out on raids. Instead he retreated to his lair like an injured beast and prepared to fight to the last with all the desperate fury of a cornered animal.

For a while his girlfriend's younger brother, a boy of fourteen or so, tried to get food, taking valuables that Baron had stolen in the hope that he could exchange them for supplies. When the boy was stopped and searched, they made him drop his trousers to see if he was Jewish. After beatings and promises that he and his sister would be saved if he showed them where Baron was hiding, he led a reinforced search party through the forest. A group of Germans surrounded the dug-out and shouted to the young couple that they should come out with their hands up. There was never any question of what would happen to them and Baron preferred to sit out a siege, which he had planned for many weeks, first shooting the Ukrainian volunteer who was sent in to get him and then tossing back a hand-grenade, which exploded in front of his attackers, wounding a couple more. Realising that he stood no chance, he then shot his girlfriend and clambered out to face a volley of bullets. The Germans shot her brother on the spot.

The two young Jews were buried in the forest, but Baron's emaciated body was hung in the centre of Modryn, bandages still dangling from arm and leg, and a notice in German, Polish and Ukrainian attached around his neck which read: 'Anyone who raises his hand against a German citizen or soldier will be punished like this murderer.' It stayed there for three days and all villagers were made to file past it.

In 1941 we were due to break up from technical school on 20 June, a Friday. For me there was a peculiar symmetry to the military upheavals: the German invasion of Poland had begun on the first day of the new term; now Operation Barbarossa began at midnight on the second day of the summer holidays. Since the end of April we had seen trains covered in tarpaulins which shrouded field guns, tanks and lorries draw into the station in Hrubieszow. Polish labourers had widened the road to the east and dug fortifications along the western side of the Bug. None of this necessarily signalled an imminent German invasion, as the military installations seemed to be designed for defence, but when tens of thousands of troops marched through the town in mid-June it became clear that they only had one purpose and that was attack.

The other school in Mirce had finished two weeks early because the Germans had requisitioned the building for use as a Divisional HQ, and it was from the headmaster's son, a classmate of mine, that I first heard that the invasion had begun. I raced home to tell my grandfather that German troops had crossed the Soviet border from East Prussia. My friend's father had heard officers discussing it, so it must be true, I told him, but my grandfather made little sign of taking the news seriously, since it came from me via a second-hand source. The following day the radio announced that panzer divisions had advanced on all fronts.

In that last week of June we watched column after column of German troops marching east. A little later there were human columns of a rather different sort being marched in the other direction. These barefoot prisoners quickly became a common sight on all the roads, as they trudged in the direction of Germany. If Polish civilians threw the prisoners scraps of food, they scrambled to pick them up, pausing only to nod thanks, knowing that should their guards see them the penalty for eating the merest morsel was death.

I remember one typical column, which, walking in twos and threes, took an hour and a half to walk past me, meaning there must have been upwards of 15,000 men. When they fell from exhaustion or because the pain from their bloody feet had become unbearable, guards shot them in the head or ran a bayonet through their stomachs. Human remains littered the countryside.

One September afternoon I was driving a cart of potatoes and sugar beet with my grandfather when we overtook a straggling line of Soviet POWs. Several of them, believing themselves to be out of sight of the guards, dived towards the raw vegetables and started to devour them in a hectic frenzy which ended abruptly with a burst of gunfire. Two or three were killed and the others stopped eating. What has stuck in my mind ever since is the way a young captain yelled to the survivors.

'Fall in! Quick march!' he ordered, as if he was still on the parade ground, and then added in a voice full of anger, wounded pride and defiance, 'We shall carry on for as long as we can. The day shall come when these murdering bastards will pay with their blood for what they have done to us.'

They still had a language which was their own and which the Germans could not understand. That was their last and only site of freedom.

The marches continued throughout the winter, through the snow and the blizzards. Their only purpose, despite labour shortages in the Reich, was to kill off the greatest number of prisoners by the most economical means. Stalin had refused to sign the Geneva Convention, so Soviet prisoners did not have even a veneer of official protection.

Soviet POWs were joined on the road by similar columns of Jews. One which I saw consisted exclusively of men, some Litvaks in traditional dress, but mostly assimilated Jews, who from their appearance I guessed to have been city dwellers, middle-class merchants and professional people rather than small shopkeepers and scrap-iron dealers. They still looked reasonably healthy and their clothes, although dirty and torn, had not yet become threadbare. Edek muttered to my grandfather that surely they knew they were all going to be killed, as scores had already been shot along the way.

'Why don't they resist, why don't they fight?' he asked, hoping for an answer from his father, who had always done business with Jews, which would account for this apparent acceptance of death.

'They've got no chance,' my grandfather replied. 'They all know it. Look in their eyes.'

It is true that there was only one guard, armed with a machine gun, for every forty or fifty Jews; it is also true that had they all acted in unison in response to a pre-arranged signal, they could have overpowered their guards, grabbed the guns and turned them on their captors.

Many people have asked the same question as Edek, wondering how millions of Jews could be destroyed in the space of a few short years. The answer is that many did fight back when an opportunity presented itself, fighting like cornered tigers in the Warsaw Ghetto. Others took to the forests to sabotage the German war effort. But in a situation like the one Edek and I witnessed, a revolt needs to be planned if it is going to succeed. Any prisoner who stepped out of the column or aroused the faintest suspicion would have been shot on the spot. Anyone who had jumped on an individual guard would have been killed before others could get hold of the guard's machine gun. It would have been impossible for would-be ring-leaders to communicate with others further down the line to get them to pounce at the same moment. A handful of armed soldiers can always subdue an unarmed crowd.

In my view what is more significant is that each individual still hoped that he alone out of all the others might survive and still harboured the thought that even if all the rest perished, he would be the one, by some miracle or quirk of fortune, to get away. After repeated beatings and the indignities of a forced march, everyone concentrates on surviving for the next half an hour because everyone thinks that something might just happen in that half-hour which could change everything. This feeling was compounded by a sense that the Germans could not possibly intend to do away with everybody, that there must have been some sort of mistake or that there must be some purpose other than the unthinkable to their having been taken away. The Germans always did as much as they could to encourage that sort of thinking and invariably promised the people they herded onto trains and rounded up to march to their deaths that they were going to a work camp or to an industrial plant where they would be looked after and could use their professional skills. They never broadcast their plans to their victims.

To anyone who asks, 'Why did the Jews let themselves be killed in that way?' I would reply, 'Why did the Poles who were led off to concentration camps let themselves be killed? Or the Soviet prisoners of war, who also counted their dead in millions?'

In Hrubieszow the Jewish ghetto consisted of a few streets fenced off with barbed wire, from which, as Hrubieszow had never had its own Jewish quarter, let alone ghetto, Polish families had been evacuated. From Edek's upstairs window I could peer over the fence and see the hundreds of men, women and children crammed inside. I recognised several of the Ukrainian militia on patrol as some of them used to come to my lodgings to drink with my landlady.

Two of them were drinking one autumn afternoon in 1941 as they played a life-and-death game with the prisoners. Each took turns to aim pot-shots at the petrified human targets who scurried from house to house to avoid the bullets, crouching behind walls and any other structure that could afford them some protection. The rules of the game were simple: if someone scored a direct hit and the other missed, the first won the bet and pocketed the money each had staked on the round. I witnessed these games three or four times that autumn and saw them kill at least thirty Jews in this way, leaving the bodies where they lay. Once it had finished, survivors dragged off the corpses for a makeshift burial. There were up to 8,000 Jews in the ghetto at that time. By the summer of 1943 it had been emptied.

When I passed very early one morning in November 1942 there were no guards to be seen, though the barbed wire was still in place. One of the few remaining Jewish prisoners called to me to ask if I had anything to eat. At first I took him to be an old man of at least seventy, but as I drew closer and looked at his features, I saw that he had aged prematurely and was probably still in his forties. From his accent I knew he came from one of the eastern counties, Volhynia or Podolia. As I always carried a crust of bread in my pocket wrapped in newspaper, I threw the small package to him over the fence. He stuffed it quickly into his coat to eat when the danger of others seeing him with food had passed, then thanked me profusely and indicated that he wanted to repay or reward me with something. As there was an abandoned boot lying nearby, an ankle-high man's boot with strong elastic instead of shoelaces, he lobbed this over to me. Somewhat baffled, I took it, nodding my thanks in return, and wandered away.

The boot was not in bad condition, and if he had given me a pair it would certainly have been worth a bit of money. It was made of good quality leather. I took it to a boy a couple of years older than me who always seemed to know how to make money from unlikely transactions and asked him how much he could give me for it. He offered me a few groschen, which I accepted. He in turn took it to his cousin who paid him two whole zlotys, ten times more than I had received, because he needed the elastic. As he was preparing to dismantle the shoe, he discovered that the heel turned. When he twisted it, out fell two gold roubles. My friend, who had been pleased with his two zlotys a moment earlier, demanded one of the roubles and, when his demand was refused, he came back to me to ask where I had found it and whether I knew where the other boot was. I saw him later pacing up and down the ghetto fence, his eyes rooted to the ground. Edek called me an idiot for getting rid of it but I replied, 'Why didn't you take it, then? I offered it to you for nothing but you said it was worthless.'

It was either at this time or shortly afterwards that I witnessed an atrocity committed against a group of Jewish children, the only one I saw apart from the columns of marching men, or those in Majdanek where they happened all day and night. A four-wheeled cart passed me in the street, pulled by a single horse and carrying sixteen Jewish children, aged anything from eighteen months to fourteen or fifteen. There were no adults among them and the older ones held the babies in their arms. They were all standing up and looking out from between the uprights of the wooden cart; the life had gone out of their eyes and it was a dull stare which met my gaze. They were skinny but not emaciated, as pale as death but not dropping from exhaustion or cut from beatings. It was their last journey and from the vacant expression on their faces they must have known it. They had been discovered in a bricked-up section of a house, connected to the outside world by a tunnel through which their protectors, who seemed not to have been caught, passed them food and water. They had been there for many months, which meant the people who had looked after them must have been both dedicated to them and well organised – one person acting alone could not have supported them in this way. I watched the SS captain directing the procession, accompanied by his smartly-dressed, adoring Polish girlfriend, gazing into his eyes with smiles of admiration. A few minutes after they had passed I heard pistol shots and then wandered down to the Jewish cemetery where they had been taken. Someone standing outside told me that three uniformed Germans had fired a couple of dozen shots and killed every single child.

3

Capture and Flight

In the late autumn of 1942 news reached us of the first massacres of Poles in our vicinity. Both had occurred about twenty miles to the south and south-west of Hrubieszow and were carried out by Ukrainians, now increasingly granted free rein by the Germans, who had burnt and razed two villages. These were the first of countless such massacres: Ukrainians slaughtered Poles and Poles responded by slaughtering Ukrainians in some sort of blood-crazed sideshow to the main carnage to the east and the Jewish extermination which had begun to take place in our midst from the moment the Germans arrived.

My first attempt to fight ended ignominiously in the summer of 1942 as I was coming up to my seventeenth birthday. I returned home, crestfallen, a mere two weeks after setting off from my paternal grandfather's estates in Zakzrouvek. At that time I still had an idea of war as an adventure since the little bits of action I had witnessed had been exciting. My cousin Marian, the son of my father's favourite sister, Aunt Sophie, who had been walking with me the day we saw the German armoured column, agreed to come with me in search either of a partisan unit fighting behind German lines or General Berling's Red Polish Army, which had now been formed on Soviet territory. The idea of walking hundreds of miles to catch up with the German divisions, whose victorious progress had at last been halted, and then crossing their lines to join the Free Poles on the other side was – to say the very least – quite hare-brained. It would have been quixotic had we been two elderly men in a previous century, our heads filled with the patriotic nonsense of a Polish Golden Age, rather than a pair of stubbornly romantic adolescents.

Marian looked to me for leadership even though he was only six months younger than me. I showed him how to tie a few belongings into a bundle and attach them to sticks to carry over our shoulders. After stealing out of the house, we made our way to the local railway station, not knowing where on earth we were supposed to be heading and not really aware that we did not know. We travelled the first stretch of the journey by train. Because, unlike me, Marian did not have student identity papers, we stowed away on a goods train, which gave the right flavour of daring to the start of our illicit and heroic escapade. We arrived safely in Lublin long before dusk.

Marian, like most Poles, had only a *Kennkarte*, a little grey identity card, which, although it had to be carried at all times, never impressed a German official. Failure to carry identity papers resulted increasingly in arrest as the Germans scoured the towns and cities for forced labour. Third-class train compartments, always overflowing with Polish passengers barred from travelling first or second class, were a favourite source of slave workers.

All that was needed to stow away was a cool head and a sense of timing. We stood on the opposite side of the track to the station platform, so as to be invisible from the station buildings once the train had pulled in, waited for the very last wagon as the train began to leave, which made it easier to slip away unnoticed once at our destination, and then scrambled aboard before the train picked up speed and laid low for the duration of the journey. This much at least we managed with consummate professionalism.

From Lublin we proceeded on foot eastwards, getting lifts from horse-drawn carts, sleeping in barns and living off raw carrots we picked in fields and fruit we stole from orchards. Because it was summer, food was plentiful, the hedgerows were in bloom and the weather gave us no problems, but Marian soon started to complain.

'We'll never get there. I want to turn back. You didn't tell me it would be like this,' he wailed throughout the third day. We split two days later: I headed for Hrubieszow and he for Zakzrouvek.

His journey home must have taken him a full ten days because all told he was away for at least two weeks. His mother spent that entire time weeping, fainting and worrying herself to distraction because he had disappeared. When I saw my father again he gave me an angry lecture, furious that I had endangered his sister's son and, more to the point, got him into trouble on my behalf. As usual he seemed unconcerned about my own welfare and what I might have been through.

'If you want to live the life of a rogue and a mercenary,' he fumed, 'then that's up to you, you go ahead. But don't take anyone from the family with you next time. God only knows what I have done to deserve such a son with no more common sense than a five-year-old.'

I did not tell him that we had wanted to fight for Poland and had set out to find the Red Polish Army. The whole idea suddenly seemed so stupid, though I was neither ashamed nor contrite, merely humiliated because I was still too young and too inexperienced to be taken seriously by my father. The next time would be different – I would go alone.

At the beginning of term in September 1942 I informed a sympathetic lecturer at college that I wanted to abandon classes because I felt that continuing with my studies amounted to collaboration after we had been put in the propaganda film about the lorries. I trusted him, knowing him to be anti-Nazi, like most of the college staff, and he understood why the film had shamed me. He asked me whether I had discussed the matter with my parents and advised me strongly against leaving, pointing out that far worse could lie in store for me. I took no notice of what he said and remained in my lodgings in Hrubieszow, wondering what I should do next. I was tough, strong and well-fed, proud and headstrong and fed up with being treated like a child.

My student papers did not save me when two Gestapo officers stopped me in the street at the beginning of October. On discovering my date of birth, they informed me that all Poles of my age were now required to join an *Arbeiterabteilung*, a forced labour brigade, and that I had no option but to accompany them. When I replied that my student status exempted me from forced labour and that I had lessons to attend, one of them curtly informed me that I was a student no longer. It was a chance arrest, not brought about because the college had informed them I had absconded, as I feared at first. Yet had I not finished my studies voluntarily, I would have been safely in the classroom at that time of day.

They took me first to a depot in Hrubieszow, where about twenty other boys of my age, some of whom I knew, were waiting. The following day they drove us to a labour camp on the eastern side of the Bug, close to the village of Krylow. It was here, not far from home, that they wanted us to work, rather than in Germany as most of us had supposed. On arrival overseers issued us with grey-green uniforms: a tunic and pair of trousers made of rough cotton, which we put on over our other clothing. No one had a change of clothes because we had all been picked up on the street. All we had with us was what we happened to wearing at the time of arrest.

The camp was surrounded on all sides by double barbed wire and guarded, unlike a concentration camp, by a single tower manned by two soldiers equipped with a swivel machine gun, which enabled them to shoot on all sides in cases of attempted escape. Over the six weeks I was there, several workers, who had either strayed too near to the fences, refused to obey an order or tried to run away while on a working party, were summarily shot. The fences, which measured roughly twelve to thirteen feet in height, bent inwards so that even with protective gloves and heavy clothing it would have impossible to climb over them. The camp was small and had been erected at speed, containing only five or six prefabricated wooden huts which served as our barracks and conformed to the standard size for German camp buildings, which can nowadays be seen at the 'museums' at Dachau, Sachsenhausen and elsewhere. In Majdanek the size and design of the huts were the same, but they had inserted four rows of bunks rather than three, thus making conditions more cramped. A small group of prisoners with an overseer could construct and dismantle everything in a matter of hours and then take the barbed wire, tower and huts on to the next site. In the six weeks I was there we were moved only once to another camp built on exactly the same lines: there must have been dozens of similar ones in the area.

At first light, or even earlier as the days grew shorter, they would take us to places near the Bug where, under the supervision of German engineers, we dug foundations for concrete pillboxes. The fortifications all faced east, which meant that already in the autumn of Stalingrad the Germans were preparing for the defence of Poland. Less than a mile separated the line of pillboxes from the dug-outs and little forts facing west towards the Reich which the Soviets had erected in similar haste and which they had quickly surrendered in June 1941. In my barracks I met boys who had spent time in other camps where they had been sent to build roads, ammunition bunkers as well as pillboxes. Some camps sounded better than ours, some worse, but no one reported that the Germans tortured the labourers as a matter of policy. Although some guards carried batons the shape of baseball bats and others hit prisoners with the butts of their rifles, our main enemies proved to be the weather and the work rather than the guards themselves.

As winter grew colder and wetter, we worked in gales and snow storms, often knee-deep in water, shovelling up sodden earth to carve out foundations for the military installations. Rain and snow penetrate clothing quickly; chest complaints which led to high fevers, pneumonia and hypothermia laid up a third of the workforce at any one time. A paramedic dispensed aspirins to the sick, as the barracks filled up with those too weak to move, let alone work. Although the conditions were atrocious, and regard for our welfare minimal or non-existent, compared with what I later encountered in Majdanek these six weeks shifting earth were a holiday. In a concentration camp they have one object in mind: to kill you. Here at least they had a practical reason for wanting us to stay alive and they fed us enough to keep us going. No one died of hunger. In the evenings we could sometimes light a fire in the stove and the camaraderie of enforced proximity and shared hardship, added to the hope that the misery would soon come to an end, kept our spirits from sinking. Yet when they told me that they wanted to keep us there for at least a year, I knew I would not be able to take it and resolved to escape and return home come what may. It would take a bit more than this to break my spirit.

The only time that escape was remotely possible was on a work party outside the camp. Any other time would have been suicidal. My example from the beginning had been Uncle Edek, whom the Germans had abducted that summer, along with six of my grandfather's prize cart-horses and best cart, ordering him to join a convoy carrying shells and ammunition to the front. We had no reason to suppose we would see him again, dead or alive, yet he returned within three weeks, which now made me think there could be hope for me.

His account of his escape sounded incredibly simple and required nothing more than a touch of daring at the right moment. He had driven his cart as far as the Pripet Marshes, some 100 miles from Hrubieszow, when his convoy had come under attack from partisan artillery and Soviet aircraft. Edek abandoned his vehicle, dived for cover and, when the bombing had ended, he simply slipped away into the bushes. His captors would have been in no mood to check what had happened to him. The conditions of war make unlikely escapes like that possible, for after the guns have stopped firing and the sound of artillery ceased to ring in the guards' ears, no one is inclined to organise a roll-call. Although I was unlikely to end up in the firing-line, I decided to seize my opportunity as soon as it presented itself. This required discretion, patience and at best a partner I could trust and who would not let me down once we had broken out. I approached a friend from Hrubieszow called

Mietek and together we decided to make a run for it.

Towards the end of November two lorries with 40 to 50 prisoners between them took us to the western bank of the river, where we were ordered once more to dig into the hard frozen ground, a not quite impossible task since the deeper you dig the less frozen the earth actually is. The site was completely exposed and a fierce wind swept across the plain. As the time of departure drew nearer and the light grew dimmer, Mietek and I hid behind a concrete wall and listened to the others pack away their shovels and clamber into the lorries. This was the moment when success or failure would be decided. The guards usually counted how many of us got into the lorry and would have searched high and low once they had discovered anyone had disappeared. We knew this but had taken a chance because of the harsh weather and the darkness and because we hoped the guards would think there was nowhere for anyone to hide on the open river bank. We continued to hold our breath as the engines started. They did not count their prisoners and did not come after us. Instead the lorries pulled away while we lay motionless, hardly daring to twitch until the rumble of the engines had died away.

Nearby we discovered an abandoned house where we slept, found warmer clothes and ate what little food the former inhabitants had left behind. In the morning we set off for Mirce where Mietek lived and where we intended to hide until the dust had settled. Then our objective was to find a partisan unit, either in the immediate area or further afield. I wanted revenge now more than ever. I also wanted to get home to my family, but realised that if the Germans decided to look for me that was the first place they would search.

The trudge to Mirce was not without its perils, and even though we tried to stick to the fields it was impossible to avoid the roads completely. That evening two Ukrainian militia stopped us and threatened to shoot us for leaving our houses after curfew. We were stupid to have risked it. They both yelled at us, first in Ukrainian and subsequently in broken Polish, calling us dirty *Lacki* (from *Polacki*, a derogatory term for

Poles). They debated loudly whether or not they should shoot us there and then. When I made a remark in Ukrainian one of them bellowed at me that I should not pretend to be Ukrainian when I was Polish.

'But what do you know?' I answered.

'You're a Haho [someone from western Ukraine], you don't speak my language.'

I then tried to sing a song in the east Ukrainian dialect in the hope he would think I came from that region. They listened.

'For God's sake, say something in German to them! They won't dare touch us then,' I whispered to Mietek. He then gestured to the writing on his tunic, now covered by layers of civilian clothing.

'*Verstehen Sie Deutsch? Arbeiterabteilung ...*'

By now we had succeeded in confusing them totally and the sergeant told his subordinate to let us go, adding that it did not matter what we were, he did not want any trouble with the Germans.

It was a lucky escape, more frightening than hiding from the guards the day before, and the second time, after the Hauptmann pointing his pistol at my head, that I felt I had eluded death by a whisker. We continued towards Mirce the next day and, just before dusk, found Mietek's family who, while relieved to see their son alive, feared that their own security might be jeopardised by our presence. They told us that the SS had rounded up 80 Polish men the previous week after the shooting of a German soldier, that the hostages had been beaten and tortured before the SS had driven them to a forest and executed them. Mietek's brother-in-law had been among them. I marvelled once more that the militia had not killed us the previous night.

This news made the walk to Hrubieszow all the trickier as the militia still patrolled in force on the look-out for the Polish assassins, even after the German revenge had been so swift and brutal. We decided to walk at night through woodlands and to zigzag our way forward, arriving in the town under the cover of darkness.

Capture and Flight

For most of December I stayed with Uncle Edek, rarely leaving the house for fear I would be enlisted into another brigade of forced labourers, or worse still be found out as an escapee. The only alternative to a life in hiding was to join the armed fight against the oppressors. This became my sole wish. I needed equipment, a rifle at the very least, before I could set out. My aunt and grandmother at the farm in Modryn steadfastly refused to tell me where they had buried the Polish army weaponry after the German invasion. They all still treated me as if I were a child.

By this time we knew that the German advance had been halted and that the Soviets and Germans were fighting a life-and-death battle at Stalingrad. In the autumn the German newsreels had predicted the imminent fall of Stalingrad and shown the bedraggled Soviet troops in control of a narrow stretch of the city in front of the Volga River. The film depicted divisions of stormtroopers and SS men in heroic poses and extolled the military virtues of the Master Race which would soon crush the resistance of the motley mixture of Slavs and Asiatics who opposed it. Two years later I saw Soviet newsreels of the same battle which showed first a shot of elite troops goose-stepping past Hitler at a pre-war parade before flashing forward to images of hungry German infantry, heads and hands covered in thin rags, shod with boots made from plaited straw. Below them was the caption: 'These are the men who reached Stalingrad.'

Stalingrad was the decisive battle of the Eastern Front: half a million German troops, the whole of the Sixth Army under General von Paulus, faced an even greater number of Soviet forces, replenished by troops from the Far East, many of whom had been transported from the Siberian steppes now that the Americans had entered the war against Japan and they were no longer needed to defend the eastern frontier. They fought for six whole months, through summer, autumn and winter, reducing everything in the city to rubble and then churning over the dust from the rubble with the power of renewed bombing. In November the Volga froze; three times the Soviet commander asked von Paulus to surrender; a third of the German troops suffered frostbite and two-thirds ultimately perished. Fewer than 100,000 out of an army which had numbered half a million eventually fell into Soviet hands. Hitler and Stalin had both staked all on Stalingrad; hatred on both sides had reached an intensity which transcended reason.

After the defeat German officers wore black armbands and their soldiers walked about as if in mourning. The spring had gone out of their step once and for all, they were no longer indomitable, but anyone tempted to think the fight had gone out of them was mistaken. But they grew all the more dogged in their increasing desperation now that they had their backs to the wall. In the past they had been convinced of the invincibility of the Master Race and barked at Polish passers-by to take their hands out of their pockets when a German officer walked past; now they had red eyes from lack of sleep, maybe even from tears.

At the beginning of December, as the Battle of Stalingrad entered its final phase, I took a train south-east to Lwow, armed only with my student identity papers and what I hoped was a cast-iron excuse for travelling. When stopped, I was going to explain in Ukrainian that my uncle and aunt had been imprisoned by the Bolsheviks during the Soviet occupation and that I was going to track them down for my sick mother. As it turned out, I did not need to use the story, but having it prepared made me feel safer.

The third-class compartments were full of shabbily dressed Polish workers with dejected expressions, not talking much to each other, never laughing. They did not carry much baggage and there were hardly any children, in stark contrast to peacetime. This made the two women in my compartment, who were speaking a very elegant form of Polish, seem oddly out of place. I listened intently to their conversation.

'My nephew speaks German without an accent,' one boasted to the other, 'you can't tell he's not German.'

'My nieces and nephews speak it with a slight accent but they are fluent too in French, Spanish, and Italian. They are so gifted with languages, which is so important nowadays.'

At the doorway to the compartment stood a young Ukrainian in a black uniform, probably Gestapo I thought, although I recognised neither the sort of hat he was wearing nor the insignia which decorated it. He had a German parabellum at his side, encased in a triangular holster, and kept his gaze fixed upon me while positioning himself so as to be able to see out on both sides of the track. He yelled periodically at passengers to get out of his way if they brushed past him or momentarily obscured his view. I did not utter a word to anyone and did my best to avoid his stare.

Lwow, with its opera house and wide streets, had been a beautiful city before the war, always outshining Lublin in terms of splendour and sophistication. The magnificent railway station, with its glass and wrought-iron roof which I had admired on school trips, was worth a visit in its own right. Some of the wealthier town houses were faced with marble up to the first floor. At one time the city had been called Lemberg, when it had been the capital of Austrian Galicia and before that capital of the Polish Ukraine under the rule of the Polish-Lithuanian kings. It now looked very dirty and unkempt, everything was coated with layers of grime and muck. The city had lost its self-respect, every street brimming with displaced persons, although nothing very much seemed to have been destroyed when the Germans captured it. It was like a once elegant man about town who had fallen on bad times and gone to seed but still retained some of his old manners and gestures among the throng of his impoverished new companions. Its once thriving Jewish community was no more; its survivors awaited their fate in the ghetto, although I had no time to explore.

As I had little way of knowing how long the train was stopping and was uncertain where it was going afterwards, I decided to get out and think about what I should do to continue my journey. Another train seemed the best bet, especially after the first ride had been so easy, but the Ukrainian Gestapo man followed me down the platform and demanded, '*Ausweis, bitte,*' before switching to his own language. I understood every word but pretended I only spoke Polish and could not follow him very well. He clearly thought I was up to something.

'Are you a spy working for the filthy Bolsheviks?'

I vigorously denied this and repeated the reason for my journey. He called someone else for a second opinion and before letting me go said in loud clear voice, not knowing that I understood him, 'We'll have to keep an eye on this one, there's something very fishy about him.'

I did not stray far from the station and in the evening jumped on a goods train headed north. This ride proved far less comfortable. I made myself a little nest in the corner of a converted cattle truck. Nobody disturbed me until a full day later when the train shunted into a siding at the small town of Brody and a voice rang out from the platform, '*Alle raus!*' A few soldiers got out with me, but no one seemed at all bothered that there had been a stowaway on board.

Brody lay more or less on my route, which made me not too displeased with my progress in the first two days, but quite unprepared for the night which now lay ahead of me. Because of the curfew it would have been unwise to venture into the town itself, where I knew nobody and was unlikely to find shelter free of charge. I went into the station waiting-room and arranged myself on a wooden bench, hoping to find some sleep and wake up to continue the journey.

I had never known such cold before, not even in the labour camp. I was wearing a three-quarter length overcoat and heavy boots, but they did not do much good and left my knees quite exposed. I never slept for more than ten or fifteen minutes at a time, waking up to defrost my legs which felt as if they were going to fall off as a result of the cold. In future I decided to stick on a train at night or, failing that, find a quiet barn in the country where nobody would see me and I could burrow into the hay or straw.

At first light there was a train east and I hopped aboard without a second thought, staying on it until the following morning and this time managing to get some rest. By the time it arrived in Zytoierz, some 150 miles east of Hrubieszow, my main problem was hunger rather than cold. I was longing for nothing more than a good hot drink, the rations I had brought with me having run out long ago.

The people in the first house I knocked at refused to give me anything, but at the second I struck lucky and the three women who lived there greeted me like a lost son or nephew. Russian Ukrainians had a completely different outlook to those further west. As a Pole I had no reason to feel wary of them – anyway I was pretending to be Ukrainian myself at this time. These people had never been pro-Bolshevik, especially after the famines of the previous decade, but most of them had quickly become anti-German. Strategically and politically this was one of Hitler's big blunders: in the Soviet Ukraine he found a disaffected population who would have joined the Germans, as they did in great numbers in the Polish Ukraine, if only the Germans encouraged them to do so. Yet because partisan actions had run parallel to the German advance and underground units continued to operate hundreds of miles behind the German lines, the Germans showed no mercy to the local population and avenged partisan attacks on villagers and other civilians. When a bridge or installation was blown up or a detachment of German troops attacked, they retaliated by rounding up what they deemed to be an appropriate number of Ukrainians, usually but not always young men, and shooting them, displaying the bodies in public to teach others a lesson. The local people's initially friendly reaction subsided.

Whether this family of women believed me or not when I explained I was looking for my brother and sister who I believed to be in the vicinity of Rostov, they gave me a bowl of steaming hot borscht and a plate of cooked potatoes with mouth-watering yoghurt, so thick that the top layer of cream could be sliced off. Such a feast was rare, to say the least, in these parts at this time and I could hardly believe that I was enjoying it. My enjoyment was dampened by the knowledge that this was likely to be my last good meal for a long time. Thereafter I lived on bread and potatoes, happy if the potatoes were not raw and the bread not hard. The women's charity can only be explained by the fact that their men had all disap-peared, either dead, hundreds of miles to the east with the Red Army, or in German captivity. I could see that they were in dis-tress but did not ask the reason because at that time everyone had a long tale of pain.

When I had finished my meal, I asked if they knew the way to Rostov and they pointed me in the right direction. I was cer-tainly not the only person on a long trek, but Rostov was at least 600 miles away. First I had a lift with some peasants on a horse-drawn sleigh. They dropped me not far from a railway line where I clambered onto another German goods train which seemed to me to be going more or less where I wanted. It turned out to be carrying war supplies to the front and had only military personnel on board, but I did not realise that as I jumped into an empty wagon.

I found a warm place to sleep out of general view, or so I thought until I was woken by German voices. I was soon noticed and I thought it best to respond in Ukrainian and told the two guards that I was looking for my lost parents who had been abducted by the Bolsheviks two years ago. Perhaps because I looked so gaunt and weak they let me go, thinking I was too young or too worn out to be involved in anything subversive. Because the locals were by now far more likely to be with the partisans than collaborating with the occupiers, it was not quite so clever to claim Ukrainian nationality to German soldiers. On that occasion I got away with it.

The further I trudged the more suspicious people became of me, the more reluctant to talk to me or help me out with scraps of food – they had next to nothing for themselves and their last livestock had been slaughtered to feed German troops. If they were lucky they might still have a meagre stock of grain they had succeeded in hiding. Sometimes I managed to beg a hunk of bread or a potato, which is all I lived on for several weeks. I continued either on foot or by sleigh when someone would give me a lift, having decided that trains were too dangerous. I felt safer on main roads. As the days passed, I started to think how in practical terms I could join a Polish unit of the Red Army. I was not interested in seeking out local groups of Russians or Ukrainians operating behind the German lines. How was I to cross the front unarmed and all alone? How could I find out the best place to do so? I dared not ask anybody I met.

Kharkov was the first major city on my route and I thought it best to bypass it. I came to a village to the south which seemed to me at first to have been completely abandoned until I saw the bodies of two dozen men hanging from makeshift scaffolds. Contrary to the custom, there were no signs saying why they had been killed. I approached a house which had wisps of smoke coiling from a crooked chimney and noticed a very old woman sitting with a young child in the doorway. I asked her who had done the killing. It was pointless to ask for food. She could not answer me, but the child simply said it was the Germans. I was only 100 miles from the front, too far away to hear artillery fire, and 200 miles from Stalingrad.

Frightened, dispirited and hungry, I wasted no time in turning back. There seemed to be no point now that I had enough time to think about what I was doing, had suffered so terribly on the long walk and now seen so many bodies hanging in the village. I went back the way I came and somehow continued to survive on the bread and potatoes I begged from homesteads, just about managing to stay warm at night in barns. The journey again lasted many days and nights, slowly turning into weeks and becoming a blur in my memory. I cannot remember much, I suppose, because of the monotony of the trudge. I did not really know where I was going until I got a lift in a German truck which finished up in a village called Stubunow, just a few miles from Kremenets where I had lived with my mother and father before the war.

I had not been consciously heading in that direction and suddenly realised that I recognised the silhouette of the onion-domed Orthodox church over the brow of a hill. The driver, a kindly looking fifty-year-old, nodded when I showed him my student papers. He gave me a cigarette which made me feel dizzy, but I thought it would have been rude to ask for food. I felt very excited and made my way directly to Kremenets where

I knew I would be all right, as I had Ukrainian friends from the old days who would put me up. I got on a sleigh and was dropped near the old base and saw the town I had known from all that time ago. It felt like a miracle to stumble across it in the way I had done.

A poor Ukrainian family which I had visited as a schoolboy had prospered, first under Soviet and subsequently under German rule, and they told me they had never had as much food and clothing as since the war started. They remembered how I had been generous to them and now returned my favours. My two old schoolmates had grown up but they were all, even the little ones, as tough as tough: the smallest brother would let himself be picked up by his hair and dangled impassively for as long as his brothers could hold him and still not issue a sound. Pietro, who had been a tearaway, had joined the Communists and was now with the partisans. They told me proudly that he was already a junior sergeant.

I was taken to see some of the surviving Polish families who had fared far less well. Polish civil servants had all been shot or deported to Siberia by the time the Germans reached Kremenets at the beginning of August 1941. The town was surrounded by hills and initially it had been bypassed by the German panzer divisions on their rush forwards. They had taken the town relatively late in the summer campaign. People told me that Herr Kacs, our Jewish butcher, had fled in broad daylight at their approach and set off across the fields on foot with Germans chasing him. He continued to run after a bullet hit him in the back; his screaming could be heard in the town. A few other Jews escaped for the time being, but there were none left now. The Germans had also shot four brothers who had arrived there in 1937 and established a lorry business. Because they were *Volksdeutsche* and the Soviets had not despatched them themselves, the Germans reasoned they must be traitors and shot them in their house. Most other citizens, as long as they were not Jewish, had not yet been killed.

I was not allowed to stay free for very long and was stopped in the street after a few days by a Polish-speaking German sergeant and a Gestapo officer, who took me back to the military camp, now taken over by the Germans. They were convinced I spelt trouble, but their attitude softened once I showed them my papers. In that respect they were typical Germans: their respect for documentation was absolute. One of them said he had an aunt who lived near Hrubieszow and I escaped with nothing worse than a clip around the ear and a sharp reprimand for being so far from home. They then said that they needed country boys to help in the stables and that they would let me off this time, 'out of the goodness of their hearts', but that if I tried anything on them again they would shoot me. When I got to the stables, which I knew well from childhood, the overseer explained that there were 100 Ukrainian boys attending to the horses and that they would tell me what I had to do.

Luck was on my side again, the job turned out to be easy and I had no intention of escaping for the time being. The work was half indoors, half outside, and by no means as strenuous as the labour camp. Food was sufficient, accommodation warm from the body heat of so many horses and the regime almost lax: most of the Ukrainians were allowed home at night. Those of us who stayed overnight slept in the same barracks that the *Ulanen*, the elite cavalry regiment, had used before the war; the stables were the same stables, in fact everything was exactly the same as before the war, except there were now only half the number of horses. I had four stallions to look after and sometimes I even enjoyed the work. I fed them their oats first thing in the morning before mucking out the stable, groomed and brushed each of them in turn and then, unless it was too cold, took each one out for an hour's exercise. I learnt how to get them to trot and to gallop at my command and tried not to let anyone notice I was not as used to this sort of work as the rest seemed to be.

The Germans let the Ukrainian boys go home at night because they knew they would never try to escape for fear their families would be punished. I happily did other people's night duty in return for extra rations. There was no hunger here. On the contrary, there was plenty of good bread which was mixed far more favourably than that I was to eat later: 50 per cent flour, 20 per cent potato mash and only 30 per cent wood from saplings. We also had salami, potato soup, even real meat sometimes, and if I did an extra night shift then I could expect a few slices of backfat brought in from the boy's family. The stables were not just warm, they constituted an oasis of heat in a desert of snow. After so many freezing nights spent huddled in a greatcoat, I appreciated that above all else. The only thing I wanted was a proper bath and a new set of clothes, but I had to make do with my old rags and washing in a basin of melted snow in the morning. 'I can stay here,' I thought to myself. It was an ideal place to recuperate after the ordeal of my journey through the Russian winter.

While on the whole we were treated well, there were some unpleasant incidents. When the officers wanted to impress their girlfriends with impromptu rodeo displays they used us for sport. While they sat at the ringside, we were sent into the arena to ride untamed stallions, newly arrived in the stables. I was once the fifth or sixth in line and was tossed off immediately by the frightened animal and had to scurry to the side to avoid his kicks. None of us lasted more than five or ten seconds, but we all knew we should try to fall backwards, as it was safer. At one of these entertainments a Cossack suddenly appeared from nowhere after a dozen or so of us had already been thrown to the ground, all of us bruised, some kicked and concussed. He leapt on the stallion and rode him until he was foaming at the mouth, sweating and breathing heavily, then eased his grip on the reins, shouted at him and gave him a pat, at which his steed stood still and let himself be led meekly away. One of the old hands told me the secret was that you must never let the horse see that you are as afraid as he is. I once saw him first yell at and then punch an untamed horse, which then obeyed him.

It took me weeks to discover why we were looking after the stallions in this way and what the Germans intended to do with them. Their planning for the future was invariably meticulous.

They had discovered that the condition of the roads in Russia, or sometimes the complete lack of roads, meant that horse-drawn transport was much more efficient in winter than motor vehicles, whose diesel could freeze at temperatures of minus 40 centigrade, as it did at the gates of Moscow and Leningrad in 1941. That was why Edek had been taken off the previous summer and why they were using Polish slave labour to build roads with clinker and logs. They were obviously intent, even now in the middle of the war, on ensuring a supply of high-quality horses. In the spring, starting at the end of February shortly after I arrived, they began to send out two or three stallions at a time, accompanied by as many keepers, to every part of the Ukraine and eastern Poland, where they would travel from village to village for the local farmers to bring their mares for insemination. That way they would not have to trust to chance or what the local population could provide but would have thousands of good young work horses each year.

The other boys talked of Kiev, Vilnius, Minsk and the Carpathian Mountains, and it was planned that the mating season should continue until July – thus next year's foals would be born between February and June. In three years' time there would be a regular and plentiful supply of horses for use in the east; no matter that three years later the Nazis would be beaten back into Germany, they planned for the long term. I began to count the days until I would be sent off and I hoped it would be somewhere near Hrubieszow. As it turned out I was not disappointed and they despatched me to a belt of villages, 30 miles from my family town. No one was sent to a more westerly location, luck was still on my side, as the area east of the Bug was where the Germans had their main problems with transport and which they made the main focus of the breeding programme.

When we set off at the beginning of March, we trotted for two to three hours at a time, slowing down for a quarter of an hour to walking pace to let the horses rest a little. A lorry with basic provisions waited for us at appointed places along the route and checked that we were still on course. Before leaving, we were told that any attempt to escape would be punished by execution and I was not stupid enough to try anything until it was safer. The snow had all but melted, everywhere was dripping wet, and so the weather presented us with few problems, but the cheap leather saddle cut right through me and every muscle in my body began to ache. My legs were so sore that I could hardly walk at the end of the day and my backside felt as if it had no flesh left on it.

The German soldier in charge of us was in his late fifties – this was not a job for young, able-bodied men – and once we had got as far as Wlodizimierz he could not really care what we did. He just wanted to get back home to his family, like the driver who had given me a lift to Kremenets. He tried once to show me photographs of his grandchildren and clearly wanted someone to talk to, but I was not interested. There was widespread hunger in this region in 1943, as there had been the previous winter, because of German confiscation of goods and livestock. In the summer the peasants had been so hungry that they harvested wheat before it was ripe. This year they would be lucky if they managed to plant any at all. Nevertheless, from all the nearby villages they brought in their mares to be inseminated by the stallions.

Escape would be simple, I thought, as we were not guarded and all I had to do was wait until my legs had recovered enough to be able to walk and then I could set off. But escape to what? I had been away for a total of four months, the war had entered a new phase after Stalingrad and the Germans were now retreating on all fronts. For Poland that meant only that the violence was about to intensify. A Pole in the village told me of fresh Ukrainian massacres of Polish civilians east of the Bug. I had no idea whether massacres had already started, or were about to start, on the western side and neither did I have an idea of what to expect if I got back home, how many of my family would still be alive.

It was a journey of only about 30 miles and I thought I could do it in a couple of nights' walking. The curfew never applied properly to rural areas and I was careful to travel at night and to stick to the fields and forests. I had a little suitcase I had picked up in the stables which contained not much more than a dirty towel and I tried to drop it to the ground if anyone saw me so as not to arouse suspicion and make them think I was just an agricultural worker plodding his way home. Once I reached the Bug, though, there was nothing for it but to cross the river by one of the bridges, and this meant confronting the German guards who were stationed on both banks.

'Hands up!' the first one shouted. My suitcase fell to the ground.

'Where are you going?'

'Hrubieszow,' I replied and there followed a few more words in German which I did not understand. I knew he could shoot me there and then if he felt inclined to do so, but something told me he was not the sort to do that. Instead he led me into the barrack room to see the sergeant who was sitting at his desk fiddling with his papers and I prayed that my student card would do the trick yet again. The German respect for documents really is unfathomable. He stared at it, noted it was stamped in Hrubieszow, then stared at me, not quite believing that anyone, even a filthy Polack, could be quite as dirty as I was. I had several months' grime ground into every pore of my face and no doubt I stank too; my clothes were black and threadbare; it had been four months since I had bathed or changed. He then opened my case and prodded around with his stick, evidently afraid of soiling his hands on what he found there. Apart from the blackened towel, I had a kilo or so of yellow tobacco leaves I had carried from Kremenets, hoping I could get some money for them somewhere. He seemed more bewildered than curious and reacted as if I represented a life-form he had not previously encountered, perhaps only read about in books.

After checking once more where I was heading, he asked where I had come from I said I had been visiting an aunt whom no one in my family had seen since the Bolshevik invasion and retreat. He accepted this, perhaps reassured that I had relatives like other human beings, but still wanted to know why I was so filthy. He then gestured in the direction of the river and, calling me a 'filthy Polish pig', suggested that I wash myself. This made me seethe with anger. I thought that if he had slept rough for as long as I had and then walked and ridden as far as I had, then he too would be filthy. He then escorted me onto the bridge, picked up the phone and informed his comrades on the other side that they should let me pass. The cross-examination had been painless and much quicker than I had dared expect. I was free to move on and not far from home, but for some reason the insult hurt me and I had difficulty swallowing my pride and anger.

Back in Hrubieszow I had two choices of accommodation: my Polish landlady with her Ukrainian lover or Uncle Edek's. My family had all survived: Kasimir, Stanislaw and Anthony were all still alive. The Germans had changed, though, and there were still lots of black armbands to mark the defeat at Stalingrad. Returning after a lengthy absence meant I noticed the decay and devastation more than I had previously. By this time there were very few Jews left in the ghetto; those who were left were too old and infirm to escape and they did not seem to be guarded properly any more.

In May my mother insisted I go to Zakzrouvek to lie low after another batch of Poles had been taken hostage and shot. My grandmother gave me a suitcase full of meat to take to my father's family, who despite their estate had far less to eat because of the German overseer. Ironically, peasants and small landowners had more food at their disposal than the owners of larger farms, say over 100 acres, which the Germans administered themselves. My maternal grandmother had plenty, as she could always declare fewer piglets to the German authorities than actually arrived in the litter. She wanted me to take my father's family more than the five or six kilos of bacon that fitted into my case.

I took the train to Lublin, where I met Aunt Sophie who was setting off for her parents' farm because of the danger posed by staying in Lublin. We found various members of the extended family in Zakzrouvek, including my five female cousins whose brother Peter had fled to join the RAF at the beginning of the war. Everyone was astounded at the quantities of fatty bacon I dumped on the kitchen table; there was enough to feed us all for more than a week. Apart from the shortages, life continued relatively peacefully in Zakzrouvek, except that the German overseer poked his nose into all our business and had effectively taken over the running of the farm, in particular the hydro-electric flour mill, from my uncles.

I returned to Hrubieszow later in the summer after partisan activity and the resultant reprisals made Zakzrouvek just as hot a place to be in as Lublin or the western Bug. I went first to Modryn and then stayed with my parents, who had moved to a hamlet on the other side of the river, away from the main road. They wanted me to stay with them where they said it was safer than anywhere else, but I could not stand my mother's nagging of my father – I thought she humiliated him and felt humiliated in his place. My wish was the same as it had been a year ago: I wanted to fight and the opportunity to do so was now not far away. The fighting came to me; there was no need to go in search of it.

4

The Ukrainian Massacres

In the forests where Baron had dug his hide-out I had a friend named Karina, a poet and an idealist, who organised a few local youngsters to attack German buildings after dark. He put me in touch with the local Peasants' Battalion, who at first told me that I was too young to fight with them. Had I had my own weapon, the story might have been different, and I cursed my aunt for refusing to tell me where the arms were buried. Instead I joined Karina's small group in order to prove what I could do. Armed with five rifles and a couple of dozen hand-grenades, we attacked a German storage depot, scaring off the sentry with a few pot-shots. We blasted off the locks and then tossed in the grenades but, although we damaged the stores of food and equipment, we failed to open a heavy safe we came across inside. That was my first taste of real action. It had been easy and I wanted more.

The next month Karina again proposed me to the local unit and they reacted more positively, quizzing me on military tactics and equipment. During the summer they sent me back to the technical college so that I would have a cover for collecting information on German troop movements in Hrubieszow. My student ID still served as a passe-partout and, despite my height, I still managed to look younger than my age. Yet I was still furious that they would not let me fight with them and took the rebuff as a personal slight. A sergeant heard me complaining and took me aside.

'Look, young fellow,' he said, 'we need every available man, also on the inside, working in the towns. You have the perfect documentation, the perfect cover. You can walk the streets without fear of arrest. That's why we're sending you to Hrubieszow. It's a vitally important job.'

His comments made me feel slightly better.

They wanted to know everything: the number of military trains passing through the station; their cargo; what insignia were painted on the military vehicles they unloaded; the nationality of the troops (German, Ukrainian, Lithuanian or Latvian) and whether they belonged to the Wehrmacht or the SS. I identified Lithuanian and Ukrainian troops by the colour of their shoulder flashes. The skull and crossbones on the SS uniforms made them unmistakable.

If I could get within earshot without arousing suspicion, I attempted to understand what the soldiers were saying to each other. The Slav languages presented me with no problems and I memorised all the details by repeating them over and over to myself. Only when there was something I did not understand, German lettering or symbols, for instance, did I make a note to show to someone afterwards. In these cases I always scribbled in the back of a school exercise book and, if stopped and questioned, planned to say that it was homework. It was imperative never to jot anything on a separate piece of paper and always to write in a rough code. If I had anything urgent to report, I jumped on a bicycle to reach the unit fifteen miles away in Laskuv. If there was a danger of running into a convoy, I did the journey on foot, weaving my way through the woods past Ukrainian villages.

I joined the Peasants' Battalion from necessity and conviction: from necessity because they were the only Polish partisans under arms in the immediate area, and from conviction because my grandfather had supported the Peasants' Party before the war. My unit had up to 350 men under the command of a pre-war NCO, a small man with narrow, steely eyes who insisted on strict military discipline and adherence to the correct military codes of conduct. Both the size and composition of the unit fluctuated with our casualty rate, which soared in the New Year of 1944, but generally speaking, in the time I fought with it, new men joined just as quickly as others were killed.

The CO trained us on the hoof, sometimes giving lectures on such basics as the correct performance of guard duty or the right formation to adopt when moving through potentially hostile territory. Some of the men continued to work on their farms by day and joined the unit for actions at night, while the rest, including myself from the autumn onwards, lived permanently in the field, sleeping in barns, forests and deserted houses, where we were crowded twenty to a room for warmth and security. We had a mixture of arms and ammunition, most of it captured from the enemy: about a dozen heavy machine guns, a handful of ancient cannons and three or four dozen sub-machine guns in addition to rifles, pistols and hand-grenades. All manner of other bits and pieces passed through our hands, as we were grateful for whatever we could find or loot from the enemy. Like our numbers and personnel, our weaponry changed constantly. If there was no dispute over who had killed a particular German or Ukrainian, then that man had the pickings of clothes, boots (always especially treasured items), helmet and other paraphernalia, though generally not the weapons, which became communal property.

At one point we were joined by two platoons of Polish police, originally sent by the Germans to fight on the eastern side of the Bug, who had deserted *en masse* once faced with what was happening to their compatriots at the hands of the Ukrainian militia. The Germans had told them that Russian and Ukrainian bandits were burning Polish villages, but when they got there and discovered the Germans themselves had in fact armed the Ukrainian gangs, they beat a path to fight with the partisans. We had some Russians with us at one time too, including a sergeant who sang in a deep, powerful voice about Brazilian beaches. The Russians had a happy-go-lucky attitude to life and kissed their dead comrades goodbye, knowing that they themselves had not long to live. A couple of Kalmuk deserters from General Vlasov's renegade army even teamed up with us for a while. They said that two of their soldiers had been killed by Ukrainians and that they wanted to fight with us instead of with the Germans.

Vlasov had deserted from the Red Army and led a couple of divisions of disaffected Soviet soldiers, mainly from the Asian and Caucasian republics. We called them Kalmuks. When they came for us in the forests they would sing, shout and cavort through the undergrowth to keep up their own spirits and deceive us into thinking they outnumbered us. The Germans avoided sending their own soldiers after partisans; they held the lives of the Kalmuks to be cheaper.

I was left behind one day with half the Polish police after the others had left to get food. Thinking ourselves too far from Nazi strongholds for the Ukrainian bands, we waited calmly for their return and when figures emerged in the distance, we assumed they were ours and went forward to greet them. But they responded to our welcome by opening up with machine guns and in a few minutes had killed twelve of our number, mainly from the police platoon. They captured a Tokarov, a valuable Russian-made machine gun, and several rifles before scurrying back over the hill from where they had come. They then regrouped to attack our flank after the main unit, hearing the firing, had given chase in the deep snow. These were Bandera's troops, Ukrainian nationalists who operated east of the Bug and were identifiable by their green uniforms and distinctive hats.

One of the police had been shot trying to run forward to hide behind a tree and reload his gun. I remember his death because I had never before seen bullets enter a man's body in freezing weather. They disappeared into his legs, his chest, his head, making tiny holes and drawing only a small amount of blood, which froze instantly on contact with the air. He lay in his uniform without an overcoat, still twitching slightly when his elder brother approached his body and bent down. There was not a tear in his eye. It was better for me not to say anything to him straightaway, even though I was standing a few feet away, but to wait until later to tell him I was sorry. He pulled out a pocket-watch, a gift from his dead brother, and held it in his hand while he declaimed his revenge to the silent forest.

'They'll pay for your death. I'll make them pay. You and I fought like civilised people, we didn't stoop to their level, we never killed children or women or unarmed men. We fired when they fired at us. From now on I'll make every Nazi and every Ukrainian pay for your death.' He kept his bloodthirsty promise.

For six months from June 1943 we roamed through the county of Lublin and took the fight to the Germans by attacking small convoys and throwing whatever sand we could into the Nazi war machine. We once blew up a whole train after capturing some explosives, but usually we lacked the munitions which would have enabled us to concentrate on the railways. Compared with the Communist cells of the Polish People's Army, which received arms from Soviet parachute drops, we were under-equipped, and compared with the Home Army, under the command of the Government in Exile in London, which by this time was organised throughout Poland, our numbers were insignificant. But we co-operated with both the Communists and the nationalists, while they refused to come to each other's aid in battle. Our aim was to liberate Poland from the Nazis with whatever means we had at our disposal.

Yet from the autumn of 1943 onwards our energies were increasingly taken up with the task of safeguarding the local Polish population from Ukrainian attack rather than with attacking the Germans. For that reason my main memories of partisan activity concern far less the acts of sabotage and the hit-and-run operations carried out against the Germans all over occupied Poland than the war against the Ukrainian Nazis, which was fought village by village, settlement by settlement. For several terrible months, until I was captured in April 1944, we fought regular and irregular Ukrainian troops, the Ukrainian militia and the Ukrainian SS, as well as the Germans, who thus succeeded in their aim of distracting partisan attention from their own military activities.

The Ukrainian Massacres

The Germans were content to have the Ukrainians do some of their dirty work for them. Smashing the Polish Resistance was one of the first priorities. We reacted to their attacks, which reached unspeakable levels of barbarity, with a ruthlessness of our own. When we overran a Ukrainian settlement, we systematically took out the men of fighting age and executed them, often by letting them run 40 paces ahead of us and shooting them in the back. That was considered the most humane method. Others in the unit, whose actions I will describe, behaved differently and exacted a terrible revenge. No one raised a finger to stop them.

While I never saw one of our men pick up a baby or small child with the point of a bayonet and toss it onto a fire, I saw the charred corpses of Polish babies who had been killed that way. If none of our number did that, then it was the only atrocity that we did not commit. What I can say for my part is that I never knowingly or deliberately killed non-combatants. Like the overwhelming majority of members of my unit, I concentrated on the Ukrainian men, who were either actual or potential armed fighters.

Some time in the late autumn two Kalmuks accompanied by a German soldier arrived in Laskuv at a homestead which functioned as one of our covert strongholds. They demanded food and drink, which they were given. After their meal the German soldier drove away, leaving the Kalmuks to finish two bottles of vodka, no doubt with the intention of returning to their base before sundown, as travelling after dark was dangerous for them. In their drunkenness their attention turned to the two young daughters of the house, who started to scream. When the Kalmuks persisted, the girls' father shot them. Had the German soldier not already left, no one would have known where the Kalmuks had ended up and they would simply have been reported missing. The next day, however, a truck carrying three or four Gestapo arrived at the homestead. Before they had time to discover the bodies, they were shot too. This raised the stakes. There was never any question that the Germans would want revenge.

In Hrubieszow I watched as Wehrmacht and SS troops assembled to find the killers. When I ran to inform the CO, he told me to eat, rest and get ready for the next day. The Germans never attacked at night.

'They'll come in the late morning, towards midday, as it will take them an hour to get here and then another hour to leave their vehicles, fan out for an attack and prepare to incinerate the village.'

He was right and at about midday two staff cars accompanied by motorcycle outriders and trucks carrying about 100 troops, a mixture of Wehrmacht and SS, came into view at the bottom of the hill we intended to defend. We had dug in just in front of the first set of houses and looked down on them as they ambled upwards, not suspecting organised resistance and certainly not expecting to be outnumbered. They laughed and joked and their commanding officer even looked rather cocky as he led his men up the hill towards us. For them it was a routine reprisal on a Polish village, one of thousands the Germans carried out all over Poland, most frequently in the county of Lublin. Our orders were clear and simple: to wait until the whole group was within 100 yards of our position and then open up with everything we had, picking them off as they scattered for cover. Although they made a sitting target, the waiting still required nerves of ice and lasted an eternity. My heart pounded in my throat: this was the first time I had participated in real combat.

One of my comrades opened fire too soon and several Germans in the first line fell to the ground as the rest retreated in disarray, not pausing to return fire until they had reached their vehicles. I quickly lost concentration in the excitement and just blasted away without taking aim. Others probably did the same, as afterwards we counted only twenty-two victims. We also captured one of the staff cars, but vehicles of any sort were as good as useless to us, as we had no fuel. We set the car on fire rather than leave it for them to reclaim later.

We then had a drink. By three o'clock the CO sent out patrols, equipped with flares, to warn us if more Germans were returning. Later we discovered a soldier hiding up a chimney in an empty house at the foot of the village. He fell to the floor, dropped his rifle and raised his hands, pleading with us not to shoot.

'*Nicht schiessen. Ich habe Frau und Kinder.*'

Usually we followed the German example and took no prisoners, but as he was a regular Wehrmacht soldier rather than a member of the SS and spoke some words of Polish, the CO hesitated. The man looked to be well past normal military age and proved willing to answer our questions. Most of us still wanted to kill him even after he had claimed to be a depot guard and not a fighting man. What swayed the CO was the German's reply when asked what he wanted from the war.

'To return to my wife and family,' he said.

Without his military insignia and helmet he looked like a peasant, like some of my comrades. 'He's just like one of us,' I thought to myself, like the German driver who had taken me to Kremenets and offered me a cigarette. Even though most of the unit still wanted to put a bullet in his head, no one dared contradict the CO. He would not pause, or so I always felt, to shoot one of his own men for disobedience and, after asking the German if he knew his way back to his depot, he released him.

The question now on all our minds was that if they took 80 hostages in revenge for the shooting of a single German, then how many would they take and shoot in reprisal for twenty-two? Yet nothing happened, there were no arrests and no one was taken. Instead the Ukrainian militia, who had already attacked Poles living in scattered settlements on the eastern side of the River Bug, now turned their full attention to the more numerous Polish population on the other side.

A few days before Christmas I set out on my own to pass a message from the unit to Karina, who still operated independently in the forests the other side of Modryn. He and his band reckoned that the main unit was too passive and that there were too many things to be done to help the hungry Poles. Baron, whom they had all known, was their hero. I left my rifle behind but put a hand-grenade into my greatcoat pocket and departed to spend the night at my grandparents' farm before contacting Karina in the morning. It was 22 December 1943, the fresh, crisp snow glistened on the open fields and I discovered I could see for a mile or two, as the light from a full moon reflected off the white ground. As I was approaching the farm through the fields, I glimpsed four horse-drawn sleighs drawing into the yard.

I was still some 400 yards away when I saw half a dozen armed men dismount from each sleigh and surround the farm building. I hid behind a haystack and watched and listened as the beauty of the evening suddenly evaporated in a burst of gunfire. I assumed they had come for Kasimir and it was clear that they expected resistance. Several more shots rang out across the fields, which were to be followed by further periodic shooting. No other sounds penetrated the cold night air from inside the farm and, after what seemed to me like several hours, the men emerged from the house and drove away in their sleighs. I had no time to count them and no way of knowing whether all of them had left at once or whether some had stayed behind. I therefore stayed inside my haystack, shivering with cold and fear. I waited until dawn to creep towards the building, unable to make out anything through the frosted windows, but as I got nearer I heard crying and then saw the front-door swinging on its hinges. The inner door had also been smashed to pieces. When I stepped inside I could not believe the amount of blood, still thick and damp and spreading over the polished wooden floors. Then I saw my grandmother and Aunt Sophie. They gradually told me what had happened.

After breaking down the door, the unwanted visitors, drawn from the local Ukrainian militia, had first dragged Kasimir into the sitting room, where they set on him with rifle butts and threatened to knock out all his teeth. They had come for both Kasimir and Anthony, but Kasimir, who was on the Nazis' wanted list, was the bigger fish and he took the worst of the punishment. They had no intention of interrogating him, as the repeated ferocity of their blows meant that he was quickly incapacitated and in no fit state to talk. 'Death to all *Lacki*,' they cried, as blow followed blow. I could hardly recognise his body when I saw it. His face had ceased to be a face: every tooth was missing, every bone broken; his jaw had sunk inwards, his nose and mouth had been ripped open and the bones in his arms, legs and hands been smashed into fragments beneath the blood-stained skin which hung from his body.

My grandmother had stayed in another room where the others, Anthony, his wife Helena, Aunt Sophie and Anthony's three daughters huddled. She prayed to a picture of the Madonna and besought them to spare her son.

'Go on, pray to your old whore and see if that saves him,' one of them shouted at her.

Once they had finished hitting Kasimir, they pushed him into a bedroom and finished him off with bayonets before firing half a dozen bullets into his body. Then they came for Anthony, who had plenty of time to make a get-away. As he knew they would have avenged his escape on the women and children, he had stayed to wait his turn. They did not use torture. Before they took him, he gave my aunt his pocket-watch and wallet, kissed her quietly on the forehead and whispered to her that she must be strong and stay alive to look after the girls. He was then led out of the room and killed with a couple of rounds.

My father arrived shortly after me. There was nothing for us to do except set about the task of cleaning up the blood. We spread hay and straw on the floor where the killings had taken place and ordered two coffins from the village. My father stayed behind that evening with the corpses after the rest of us had left for Hrubieszow, where the funeral was to be held the following day, Christmas Eve. Kasimir and Anthony were buried next each other. On the way to the church my heart filled with hatred for the Ukrainians and I swore to avenge my uncles' deaths. Kasimir had been like a father or elder brother to me: he had taken me horse-riding, taught me how to ride a bicycle and always found time to answer my childish questions. If they had shot him cleanly, I thought, it somehow would not have hurt me as much, but I had seen the remains of his huge frame reduced to a mess of blood and bones. I had seen what used to be his face.

Afterwards I accompanied Sophie to call on my former land-lady to collect a few things and ask her if she knew the whereabouts of a particular friend of mine, as I had a message for him. Her Ukrainian captain sat there, already swigging vodka, as the two of us stepped inside. Even after all the crying and the agony of seeing her brother killed, my aunt's face turned even whiter when she saw the Ukrainian. She stopped herself from fainting in the doorway and, unable to speak, tugged at my sleeve to pull me away. Waving her finger from side to side in a gesture of refusal, she said that she would wait outside. As I returned, the lieutenant roared to his mistress to hurry up.

'Who's that you've got with you?'

'Just one of the boys who used to live here. He's forgotten something,' she replied and then gave me my friend's new address.

I hurried outside to my aunt.

'Quick. I want to get away from here,' she mumbled.

'What's the matter?' I asked.

'That man. The one who was sitting with her. He's the one. He's the one who said, "Pray to your old whore." He was in charge. He killed your uncles.'

I gently led her away.

During the day the captain led the town militia and at night he teamed up with the murder gangs. That was how close we lived to one another. On the evening they killed Kasimir and Anthony, the Ukrainians had continued to the next Polish vil-lage and murdered five more men, dragging them from their beds and shooting them. A sixth man, who had bullets blasted into his neck, hip, chest and stomach, survived because the cold of the snow slowed down the flow of blood.

I took my aunt to the house of a friend who was looking after her nieces and, pretending that I wanted to chase up the man whose address I had just been given, I set out to rejoin my unit. It was a walk of only fifteen miles and I was there in the early evening. My platoon sergeant told me that he was sorry to hear what had happened to my uncles and regretted that they had not been there to help. I nodded and sat down with the others to drink vodka. Everyone knew that something was going to start. At nine o'clock we moved on towards Modryn, where the CO assembled the platoon leaders to issue orders.

'Don't burn, don't loot. Just shoot young, able-bodied men. If anyone resists, make sure you shoot him before he shoots you. We have to teach them that they cannot take out selected Polish citizens and kill and torture them. We must teach them that they can't get away with that.'

They had killed seven men two nights previously; that night we killed sixteen of theirs, including an eight-year-old schoolboy. He died accidentally when a house was stormed and shots were fired through the door. He had got in the way; it was a mistake. There were 300 of us in all and we met with no resistance and suffered no casualties. Most of us knew many of the people in Modryn, so we knew who was a Nazi supporter and who was a Ukrainian nationalist. We picked them out.

A week later the Ukrainians responded by wiping out an entire Polish colony, setting fire to the houses, killing those inhabitants unable to flee and raping the women who fell into their hands, no matter how old or young. This had been the pattern of their behaviour east of the Bug, where tens of thousands of Poles had been either expelled or murdered. We retaliated by attacking an even bigger Ukrainian village and this time two or three men in our unit killed women and children. Some of them were so filled with hatred after losing whole generations of their family in the Ukrainian attacks that they swore that they would take an eye for eye, a tooth for a tooth, and they were as good as their word. I felt no remorse for my part in what happened: this was war and revenge at last. The Ukrainians in turn took their revenge by destroying a village of 500 Poles and torturing and killing all who fell into their hands. We responded by destroying two of their larger villages. They then gathered their forces for an all-out attack on a further five Polish settlements. By this time they had been joined by a regiment of German-trained troops from east of the Bug where they had finished their work in the camps and ghettos.

This was how the fighting escalated. Each time more people were killed, more houses burnt, more women raped. Men become desensitised very quickly and kill as if they knew nothing else. Even those who would otherwise hesitate before killing a fly can quickly forget they are taking human lives. In fact, in order to kill it is necessary to forget that the victims are human; as soon as eye contact is established, it becomes difficult to pull the trigger. On both sides teenagers were the worst perpetrators of atrocities.

Special treatment was always meted out to women. Rape is the male conqueror's instinctive privilege, his way of defiling and possessing his victim, and killing and sex are thus intertwined. Polish women who had slept with the enemy would not simply be shot as male traitors were: their executioner first shaved their pubic hair in front of a crowd of male onlookers. I remember one occasion when the man ordered to carry out the shaving wiped his razor after each stroke. Each time he put his fingers to his nose and said, 'This one smells Austrian,' 'That's Ukrainian,' 'I think that one was Lithuanian.' Those of us watching his performance laughed out loud: it was good theatre and we felt that these women had got what they deserved.

We moved through three Polish villages twenty-four hours after a Ukrainian attack. Houses and ruins still smouldered; charred bodies littered the ground in front of the buildings; the corpses of small children, who had been thrown onto the burning roofs, now lay where they had fallen, their heads smashed open. Those who had tried to flee lay further afield where they had been killed by bullets. They were the lucky ones. The handful of survivors had either run away or hidden in dug-outs which had escaped notice. These were usually dug in gardens behind people's houses and covered with planks and undergrowth. As a rule they were tragically easy for the attackers to locate: all they had to do was to trample on the ground to discover where it gave way. Usually they opened the hatch and threw in a grenade, moving on without bothering to inspect the damage. We shovelled in some earth to bury the remains of the victims when we found them later.

The naked remains of women often showed signs of mutilation – their vaginas had usually been slit open. Even small girls had been carved with knives and bayonets. I remember the body of one woman which lay uncovered, a nightshirt clutched in one hand, on the threshold of a burnt-out house. Yet apart from the caked trickles of blood on her legs and a few minor cuts, she looked unharmed, her face had a peaceful expression and I could see no bullet wounds. I wondered how she might have died and, almost nonchalantly turning her body over with my boot, watched her long brown hair part at the back of her skull and her brains splash to the ground from a cavernous hole. We dug a few graves and carved the number of bodies buried in each onto makeshift wooden crosses. Many remained unburied.

When we came across a pile of Ukrainian bodies the following day, one of the younger partisans named Polecat took a wooden stake he found lying at the roadside and with all his strength shoved it up the backside of one of the corpses. It was no business of mine what he did, he lived for blood and what he did to the living was far worse. Yet later I regretted not having stopped him because I realised that any Ukrainian who found the body would assume that the man had been impaled while still alive. I did not say anything to Polecat, nor stop him on other occasions, because he would have thought me weak.

The question for us, after walking through the three devastated villages, was how to get the Ukrainians once and for all and prevent them from carrying out further atrocities. To do this we had to wipe out their main bases, two heavily fortified villages some ten miles apart, which we had hitherto considered impregnable. The CO had sent messengers to the Home Army partisans further west, asking them for firepower and reinforcements. After telling us repeatedly in leaflets and hand-delivered messages not to loot and not to torture the civilian Ukrainian population but to concentrate on the German enemy, they now sent us 2,000 of their own men, who were in the main better armed and better trained than us. This was our first joint operation. It obviously made military sense to the Home Army to neutralise both villages, since Polish citizens were under threat.

The first had been a Ukrainian village with about 1,000 inhabitants before the fighting and now served as one of the two bases for Ukrainian operations, sheltering as many as 1,000 well-armed soldiers from the SS and the Nazi police and militia. It was here that they retreated after laying waste to our settlements. We needed to knock out both these village bases if we were to put more than a temporary halt to the slaughter. They lay ten miles apart and our plan was to take both on the same night, thus not allowing one to come to the aid of the other. I took part in the attack on the second village with half the combined forces. We easily outgunned them and the operation was a pushover. We bombarded the buildings with mortars the Home Army had brought with them before moving in to mop up the resistance at first light. At the end of thirteen hours of fighting, which began at ten in the evening and continued unabated until most of the Ukrainians had perished, little remained standing. Our orders were to kill all the men we found who were capable of carrying arms. There were no orders as regards non-combatants and those in the unit thirsty for more blood knew that they could kill and rape who they wanted and how they wanted. The Ukrainians were doing even worse to our people.

Polecat was always after women – old women, young women, middle-aged women, it did not matter to him. He raped them first and then killed them with a bullet to the head. Together we came across a girl of about sixteen. He was about to go for her when I stopped him.

'No. You've had your share,' I told him, 'I haven't had one yet. It's my turn.'

She was very pretty and something about her seemed familiar to me, which is why she had caught my attention. He relented and muttered something to the effect that he hoped I would enjoy myself. He would get a girl for himself from some-where else. For the moment she was completely in my power and I could see that she would do anything to stay alive for even half an hour longer. It is natural to submit without resistance in these circumstances, hoping to avoid a fate worse than rape. I grabbed her by the arm and led her off towards the trees away from the fires which had lit up the night skies and were still burning fiercely. I wanted privacy, unlike my friend who liked nothing better than to show off his virility in front of a crowd of cheering onlookers.

For some reason I asked her what she was called and when she told me I gradually realised that I probably knew her family, at least her father, and that I had possibly seen her when she was younger. I asked whether her father had owned a mill and she said that he had. It had been a primitive stone mill where my grandfather had taken his rye to be ground. I asked her again so that there could be no mistake and now I knew that we had seen each other when we were both children. We had reached the trees by this time and she had already lain down on the ground and begun to prepare herself for me. I began to think that I was not an animal, that I did not have to do what others did, and that I could let her go without Polecat seeing. I was afraid he would tell the others I was a gutless coward.

'Get up and walk a little further on,' I said to her. 'When I give the word, run for it. A few moments later I will fire a shot over your head. I won't hit you.' At no price did I want Polecat to know that I had not raped and killed her, not just because of what he would think of me but because of what he would undoubtedly do to her if he caught her. 'God bless you,' she said in Polish, and then, in Ukrainian, 'May your life be as good as you are.'

'Beat it!' I shouted and she fled into the night.

One man in our unit, a survivor of Ukrainian torture, had no fingertips left. Each one had been severed, leaving rough stumps where his nails had been. He hobbled as a result of smashed feet, and when I watched him wash one morning I saw scars on every part of his body. As he very rarely spoke, I never discovered what had happened to him, but it was said that he had lost his entire family. He was one of the few who seemed entirely fearless in his savagery and I saw him murder indiscriminately. He once buried a hatchet in the head of an old woman who had answered him back as he looted her house. In the weeks immediately after my uncles had perished, I understood why and felt no disapproval.

Like Polecat and another man I shall call Jackal, he took a certain pleasure in what he did. They all rose to the challenge of murder. I once saw them capture a towering, thickly built Ukrainian who barely flinched after Jackal had struck him on the head with a rifle butt and who still kicked and writhed on the ground after they had pumped two bullets into his chest.

'Look at him. He's a strong bastard. I bet he's killed more Poles than he can count,' Jackal shouted.

That was the thought in our minds: we were getting revenge for what they had done to us. The man still twisted and groaned after another two bullets had landed in his stomach. He was clawing the earth which had turned red with his blood. He was built like a bull and he died like a bull, still stirring after they had fired another three bullets into his body. In all he took a quarter of an hour to die as they analysed and wondered at his last responses. The vast majority in the unit did not kill for the sake of killing, yet we let the likes of Jackal and Polecat do as they pleased.

Jackal lived only for revenge. Apart from Polecat, his junior by ten years, he was the greatest torturer I came across on our side. His own life had ceased to mean anything to him after he had lost his sister and his brothers, his parents, his wife and his three little daughters in a raid. He continued to exist solely for the purpose of killing and torturing Ukrainians. I often noticed that he did not bother to take proper cover when we were under fire. He just slouched to the ground and had no fear in his eyes. He was content to die after he had killed enough Ukrainians.

Once we overpowered two Ukrainian machine-gunners who had been holding out from the first storey of a barn, keeping

100 of us at bay for more than a hour. They had a huge Spandau machine gun, a type we coveted, but by the time we got to them, one had already shot himself and the gun was nowhere to be seen. Twenty of us searched in the straw, in the outhouses, in the undergrowth and the snow for at least an hour, but we could not find it. We even checked the walls and the floorboards. The surviving Ukrainian was stoutly built, six feet tall and strong. He wore an SS uniform. Jackal and a couple of assistants stripped him to his long-johns and set on him with wooden clubs, first beating the soles of his feet until the skin peeled off and his flesh came away in chunks, then hitting him in the chest to break his ribs.

Jackal was visibly excited and impatient to inflict more pain. Still his victim would not talk. Soon he was beyond talking altogether. Jackal then put the man's fingers into the crack of a massive iron door and closed the door to break the fingers, which snapped audibly. Jackal was sweating heavily by now and set to work on the protruding fingers with a blunt iron bar. It was clearly a challenge to him to hack them off with as few blows as possible. The first three came off quickly, leaving the smallest to dangle by its last two sinews. It refused to budge and this clearly angered the torturer. It was neither a methodical nor an efficient way of inflicting pain, and the original objective of discovering the location of the Spandau had long been forgotten. At first the man had been screaming for all he was worth, but gradually his screams grew fainter until he was barely whimpering, his body jerking slightly, his voice quivering each time Jackal struck.

I moved away and by the end Jackal was alone with him as the others had let him take over. After he had finished, the man's face was a mess and his chest had collapsed, yet still he managed to emit faint sounds as Jackal dragged him to the stairs by his legs, hurled him to the bottom and pulled him away to finish him off behind the barn with a bayonet.

After all that I had seen, I could not watch as Jackal hacked at the man's fingers. Somehow, somewhere inside me, Ukrainians were more likely to provoke feelings in me than

Germans. It was not exactly compassion, perhaps more a spark of respect for human life. I would have hit the man to extract the information, which was important to us, and I would not have hesitated in shooting him once it was over. But I would not have tortured him for the sake of torturing him. My hatred was not as intense as Jackal's.

Once the two Ukrainian strongholds had been destroyed, much of the mass slaughter ceased, at least as far as my unit was concerned. We now moved north to the region round Sobibor, where, after the concentration camp had been closed in the autumn of 1943, gangs of trained Ukrainian guards had been assigned to the militia. Our aim was now to clean up the remaining armed bands of Ukrainian Nazis in order to protect the local Poles from further attacks and to enable us to get on with the job we had originally set out to do. We now had the initiative.

I remember guard duty on a cold, moonless night. The sergeant had picked me for the first stint, as he nearly always did, because I was still the youngest. Although we had no reason to feel in immediate danger, I grabbed my rifle and stared into the darkness. Suddenly the nocturnal quietness was disturbed by rustling in the undergrowth.

'Stop or I'll shoot!' I shouted. The rustling stopped. I decided after several minutes that it must have been the wind. When the next man came on duty at the end of my hour, I told him what I had heard and then disappeared to get some rest. Moments after I had fallen asleep, he was firing into the forest, as the whole company scurried into position and waited for an attack. Once more nothing stirred. We spent the rest of the night in a state of anxious anticipation, even though the noise had clearly been made by an animal or a sudden gust of wind in the branches.

The following morning the women paramedics had started to serve ravioli with cheese and meat for breakfast when news came of an attack that night on a Polish settlement. I burnt my fingers trying to grab mouthfuls of food as the unit abandoned breakfast and rushed to cut off the Ukrainian retreat. The village was small and the Ukrainians had burnt only one end of it, but 100 Polish civilians had still paid with their lives. We reckoned the Ukrainians numbered fewer than 100: we had more than three times as many men. While the paramedics treated the wounded as best they could, most of us moved to the next Ukrainian settlement and torched it. The majority of the inhabitants had taken to the forests by the time we had got there. We rampaged in the direction of the river, burning each village and farmstead we passed through and killing the men they had left behind to defend their property.

A mother who had stayed behind with her grown-up son begged me to spare him. She grabbed my boots and kissed my feet and cried in Ukrainian and Polish.

'Spare my son. He's not killed any *Lacki*. He's a good boy, my only son. Think of your own mother, think of what she would feel if she heard you'd been shot. Spare him!' Something gave way inside me this time, as I watched her writhe on the ground in front of me, telling me what a good man her son was, how he had done well at school and how she and the family depended on him. Usually I would have shot any Ukrainian at my mercy and kicked away his mother without a second thought. This time I suddenly realised that I did not want to do so and once more the thought of others finding out my cowardice and calling me soft made me afraid. I wanted my comrades to trust me and respect me: killing was the only way to earn their respect. Several of them were nearby, though out of earshot in the general clamour of gunfire and not looking in my direction. An execution was too commonplace to arouse any interest – a rape might be different, then they might creep up and laugh and joke. I was on my own.

'Get off my feet, you bitch!' I yelled at her before marching her son off to a spot by some trees a couple of hundred yards away. Unlike his mother, he did not beg. He seemed resigned to his fate. I told him to run. He obeyed and I waited for him to cover ten yards before aiming a bullet at his hip. He was so close I could hardly miss and he fell to the ground, where he lay flat on his face, not moving a muscle. As I turned him over with my boot, I saw his eyelids flicker and I quickly checked his heart, before taking his Polish army belt and going through his pockets. I then positioned his body so that the hip wound was clearly visible. I told nobody that I had not killed him and I knew that his mother would run out to find him and take him home to bandage his wound.

In the third or fourth village that morning Polecat and I found warm food on a stove in one of the houses and a half-full bottle of cherries soaked in spirit. The cherries on their own would have been enough to get us drunk, as we had eaten only a few mouthfuls at breakfast. Now we drank half of what was left in the bottle and consumed the half-cooked meal.

In the next village I got lost in another house, still drunk, as I rummaged through the trunks in a bedroom. I must have been in a stupor because I took an alarm clock, thinking I needed it to make sure the others did not cheat me on guard duty. Most of all we needed clean, fresh clothes because our own were crawling with lice. I began to pick myself out something to wear. Before I had finished running my hands through the material, I realised the roof was burning. Smoke began to fill the upstairs room. I staggered towards the door, unsure of the way to the outside, as a man dropped on top of me from a hatch in the ceiling, knocking me to the ground as he fell. We struggled for control of my rifle as I tried to parry his blows and screamed for help. The others had moved to the far end of the village by this time, not knowing that they had left me inside the house when they had set it on fire.

By the time they heard me, my assailant had very nearly beaten me unconscious and prised the rifle from my grip. All the time the smoke grew thicker and thicker, my screams hoarser and hoarser. At a point where he had all but overpowered me and I had begun once more to stare my own death in the face, the door burst open and my attacker got a bullet in the head. Polecat, who had ignited the house, had realised his mistake and brought others back to rescue me.

As the Ukrainian was sitting astride my chest when the bullet entered his skull, my face was splattered with his blood and brains. A paramedic helped me to wash and found me a change of clothes. My drunkenness had evaporated in an instant.

Later that day I refused to shoot an old man who emerged from his house which I had just helped to set ablaze. On seeing the flames begin to lick up the walls of his wooden home, he howled like an animal, waved his hands above his head, fists clenched, and danced a frenzied dance, pounding his feet on the ground as he jumped, hopped and skipped into the air. I had seen nothing like it and wanted to run.

'Shoot him, Lotnik,' a sergeant ordered me. I looked away and pretended not to have heard.

'Shoot him! That's an order,' he repeated.

'I'm not shooting an old man,' I shouted back without turning round to face him.

'I'm telling you for the last time to shoot him. That's an order.'

'You can fuck yourself,' I told him, daring him to shoot me for disobedience.

Instead he pulled out his pistol and shot the old man himself.

We continued to burn villages for about twelve hours, finding mainly abandoned settlements and meeting no organised resistance. By setting the last village alight once darkness had fallen we exposed our left flank to attack, not thinking that there might be a danger. Suddenly mortar salvos rained down in rapid succession, hitting us with a dozen shells in a few seconds. Our attackers were Ukrainian regulars near the site of Sobibor on a bend in the River Bug. We lost about ten men and then retreated. It had been sheer carelessness on our part not to send out patrols to check the countryside. We spent that night in a large country house before moving gradually back to Laskuv.

We lived in fear of capture, saw our friends get shot and blown up at our sides and had no doubt that our adversaries would show no mercy were any of us to fall into their hands. Our deaths would be as slow and painful as they wanted to make them. Fear of what they would do to us undoubtedly influenced our actions. Fear of death when under fire is different, as there is no time for reflection in the scream of battle. Fear helps to pump adrenalin and if there is time to think of death, then it can have the opposite effect to panic. In fact there can come a point when fear can go no further, when the thought of death is even comforting and its proximity gives a feeling of relief. Until that point is reached there is always the hope of surviving, the thought that help might come in the nick of time or that the enemy might give up after running out of bullets. Hope is the last casualty in such a situation and the last power you hold over your attackers is the power to take your own life, thus to decide yourself how to die and when to die, denying them the pleasure of killing you. Each of us kept a special bullet, tucked safely into a top pocket, which we took out for regular polishings.

I once had occasion to use mine, but my rifle failed to go off after I had inserted the barrel into my mouth and prepared to welcome death's liberating embrace. Fear of death was then replaced by fear of continuing to live. It was ten o'clock in the morning, the firing had continued unchecked since dawn and I knew that the Ukrainians had me surrounded. Suddenly I looked up to realise that there were just two or three of us left from a contingent numbering about 50. Our three machine guns had fallen silent, one after the other, and all I could hear was the occasional staccato round of rifle fire from our remaining handful of positions.

The main unit had moved west from our base near Laskuv the previous evening, leaving the rest of us to await the return of the CO and twenty others from a raid to recover a radio transmitter. The Ukrainians had surprised us at daybreak. We had barely enough time to scramble out of the two houses where we were sleeping and spread out in a line in front of the forest when they attacked. In the evening we had been singing and joking until midnight, vodka had passed from hand to hand until the others had set off on their raid and we settled down to sleep, twenty to a room, our boots on as always, our rifles clutched to our chests. We were ready to fight even as we slept: 30 seconds were all we needed to spring into action. A sentry sat at each door, beyond the two houses under a tree stood another and every hour on the hour the alarm clocks sounded and the guard was changed. When we heard firing towards dawn, two men went to investigate, expecting to find the CO.

They searched and listened, as the Ukrainians, unsure of our numbers but undoubtedly aware they had discovered our stronghold, spread out silently, cutting off our escape routes into the forest. Unfortunately, we were not under unified command and had made the mistake of occupying two separate houses placed 50 yards apart, which made them impossible to defend. The Ukrainians' phosphorous bullets soon shot them into flames. We had time to scramble outside into a line level with the forest, five to ten yards apart, and dig into the deep snow before the shooting started. Bullets skidded off the bark of trees and felled branches, mortars created white craters splattered with blood and equipment and turned up the earth beneath the snow. Two or three of our men, who had attempted to run for the forest, covered only a few yards before being mown down. Our attackers concentrated on the three machine guns, each manned by two or three men, and took out each one in turn. They knew they had time on their side, that there was nothing for us to do and nowhere to run, and so they kept their cover, not risking an all-out attack which would have incurred losses on their side.

At the beginning I knew I had 120 rounds for my rifle, but had no time to count the bullets as I fired them. Not until I had fired the last did I realise that help was not at hand, that only a couple of my comrades were left, and then the thought came to me that I had to use my special bullet. Fear turned to relief that it would soon all be over.

The difficulty of shooting yourself rather than someone else with a rifle can be put down to the length of the weapon, which makes it hazardous to aim the barrel at the head while still holding a finger to the trigger. It is far easier to wound or maim yourself. The secret, I had been told, is to manipulate the trigger with your right foot, while steadying the barrel with both hands. With heavy boots in freezing weather this meant that I had to place the leather strap from the ammunition pouch across the trigger in order to lever it with my feet. I found a comfortable position which enabled me to do this, leant back and aimed for my whole head. I felt at peace and completely relaxed. Then the trigger clicked and I felt I was beginning a journey to another world, but nothing had happened. I opened the bolt, checked the bullet and closed the bolt. It clicked again.

My inner peace now gave way to despair and panic. The deepest, most unnatural fear gripped my body, as my thoughts froze and mind refused to function. In disgust and anger I threw down the rifle and saw it all but disappear into the snow. But as I watched this happen, hope replaced despair and an idea began to form in my mind. If the rifle disappeared into the snow, I reasoned, this meant the snow at that point was possibly deep enough to hide a human being. There must be a ditch or trench underneath, as elsewhere the snow was barely more than half a meter in depth. Hurriedly, I tugged out the rifle and began to push beneath the frozen top crust to the soft, powdery snow below. I began to dig with the barrel, then, using my hands and arms and wriggling my whole body, I burrowed into the snow, kicking up great mounds behind me and edging forward, still gripping my rifle in front. After I had got down five or six feet, I pushed the rifle up to the surface, thinking at first that I would have to breathe through it before I discovered it was quite possible to breathe at that depth in snow. By wriggling my shoulders a little more, I made myself a hole large enough to turn round and soon discovered that I could make out voices and movements on the surface.

The Ukrainians arrived, fired a few shots, shouted at one another and evidently thought nothing of the disturbed snow above me. All around me holes had been made in the hard frozen crust, either by grenades and mortars or human beings. The Ukrainians quickly disappeared, but I remained too frightened to risk poking my head out from beneath my thick protective blanket. Now the cold took over and crept up my

body from its extremities, like an invading army taking posses-
sion of ever more bits of territory, consolidating its grip before
moving on further. My limbs grew stiff, my body temperature
gradually sank and my mind began to wander. My memory of
what happened next is hazy. I can say that I do not recall
drifting off towards death as I remained aware of where I was.
Perhaps that would have been the next stage, which my rescuers
spared me. Early in the afternoon I must have heard voices
again, this time speaking Polish, and after I had pushed the rifle
upwards and waved it with what remained of my strength and
shouted, they approached me and shouted back.

It did not take the twenty returning partisans long to dig me
out and put me on a stretcher. After recapturing the transmitter,
they had returned as planned to find just two survivors. The CO
cursed and swore, blaming himself for leaving us unprotected,
and tried to ask me what had happened. The bodies of the rest
of the company lay where they had fallen, as the Ukrainians had
not bothered to dispose of them, and were now hastily buried in
a mass grave on the edge of the forest outside Laskuv.

A paramedic removed my boots to find my toes blue with
frostbite, then rubbed my limbs first in snow and then with
methylated spirits. She exercised my legs by moving them back
and forth before wrapping me in blankets. It took me a full ten
days to recover enough to be ready for action again. Something
in my attitude changed after this experience, which has haunted
me as much as any other, as I had prepared myself mentally for
death and become convinced that I had a few seconds left, then
saved myself by diving into my grave only to be fished out before
my eyes closed for the last time. A feeling of unreality which had
enveloped me after I had decided to use my last bullet never
completely left me. Even if it eased for a while and I began to
push the memory to the back of my mind, I knew it would return
during the next attack or ambush. Sometimes I felt no fear, as if
all my fear had been used up and my capacity for dread was
exhausted. I thought that nothing could happen to me, that I
was no longer of this world. Part of me died in Laskuv.

5

In the Puszcza Solska

The great expanse of forest and marshland called the Puszcza Solska extends over most of the south of the county of Lublin and reaches as far as the Carpathian Mountains and the Romanian border. Throughout the first half of 1944 the area saw heavy fighting. Poles still lived in the tiny hamlets and villages, sometimes undisturbed by the war which raged in the world beyond. We relied on the patriotism of these peasants for food and shelter, for transport and various bits and pieces of equipment. It was very rare that they had to be persuaded to give us what we required.

The unit continued to replenish and reinforce its numbers, attracting volunteers from all walks of civilian life, all motivated to fight the Nazi terror either from conviction or because they had suffered at the occupiers' hands. In addition, small independent groups of partisans joined us; at its height the unit numbered no fewer than 700.

One day in late winter two Silesian Poles carrying rifles and ammunition stumbled into our encampment. They had broken out of a German gaol, they told us, and fought with a band of Home Army partisans who had all been killed in a devastating ambush. One displayed a wound, which was at least six months old. They proved useful, willing comrades, always ready to fetch and carry, always the first to volunteer for extra tasks. They boasted to me of their sexual conquests and their tales of resistance in Western Poland gave us renewed hope. On the day of their arrival they approached the CO with intelligence concerning a small shunting station a few miles from Zamosc, where, they claimed, the Germans had stored half a trainload of rifles, hand-grenades, explosives and assorted weaponry ready to be transported to the front. They had picked up the information in the village itself before setting off to find a unit which could take advantage of it. The German guards numbered no more than a dozen and the train was likely to be there for up to a week, if their sources could be trusted.

The NCOs grew excited – with that sort of firepower we could start knocking out entire railway stations, not just individual trains – but the CO reacted suspiciously. It sounded too good to be true. Nevertheless, he set a provisional date two days ahead for the raid, while, unbeknown to our new recruits, sending out a reconnaissance party to check the details. We kept a close watch on the pair of them, and sure enough one disappeared during the night. After losing the local man ordered to tail him, he returned at dawn, unaware that his absence had been noticed. The CO's suspicions were confirmed: what else could he have been doing except informing the Germans that an attack was planned? The scouts reported that they had located the consignment of munitions, but that the station was crawling with German troops.

We still wanted to be absolutely sure of their treachery, and on the evening of the planned attack a group of 50 men departed, to the visible dismay of the Silesians, who had expected the whole unit to move. Both then made attempts to leave, saying they wanted to take some air or go for a walk, but we told them to wait to hear the good news. For the first time they became suspicious of us. After a bruised and battered comrade staggered back in the morning, pretending to be the sole survivor from the original 50, and reported that they had been ambushed and that the entire group had been wiped out, the Silesians sang like canaries. Even though we despised traitors from our own side even more than German or Ukrainian Nazis, Jackal kept himself under control with all non-Ukrainians and he just roughed them up a little before they told us about the network of *Volksdeutsche* working with the Gestapo and the Ukrainian militia against the Polish Resistance. After Jackal had taken the boots which one of them had been wearing, the rest of us divided up the remainder of their equipment. The following day someone offered me a spare ammunition belt and I was told to shut up and not ask daft questions when I enquired what had happened to its previous owner.

We did not shoot German women we captured in combat. One day eight or nine nurses dressed in white hats and Red Cross armbands tumbled out of two lorries after we had attacked a convoy. Rather than let them go and reveal our whereabouts, we took them prisoner and confiscated their medicines and equipment. There were already about a dozen Polish women paramedics with us who neither fought nor carried guns, instead preparing food and tending the wounded. Some had a lover and protector in the unit, and two became pregnant during the winter. The senior partisans now shared out the German nurses among themselves, just as if they were booty. They stayed with us for more than a week before the CO ordered that they be marched in the direction of a town patrolled by Germans. We showed them the way and let them go. They would not have been able to say where we were headed since the bulk of the unit had disappeared and we were on the move.

One remained with us a while longer as she had learnt some Polish after falling for the handsome brute who had picked her out. But even though her surgical skills had proved very useful to us, there was no way we could trust her. The CO asked her lover whether he was prepared to be responsible for her in an emergency, by which he meant that he might have to shoot her. He replied that someone else would have to take care of that.

In the late autumn of 1943 I had been sent to convalesce with a poor family who lived in a tiny village buried deep in the forest. My chest had been crushed and two ribs fractured when my cart had run over a landmine and hurled me twenty feet into the air. I got off lightly, as the lad next to me was more badly wounded and our two horses had to be destroyed. In fact, for a split second I felt not so much as a scratch. Then a section of the front wheel dropped onto me, pinning my body to the ground until help arrived. The fortnight I spent recovering away from the unit was an oasis of peace. I ran around with a local girl and roamed in the woods, but I soon got bored and wanted to get back to the others once my fractured ribs had healed.

We were now constantly on the move in the Puszcza Solska, staying in abandoned houses and barns or, when we could find no better shelter, grabbing fitful moments of sleep sitting upright in the branches of snow-covered trees. We all lived for the moment, not expecting to be alive the following week or month, let alone the following year. This can provide a canny young soldier with an effective ploy with the opposite sex. If you tell a girl that you may be dead tomorrow or that you have had a premonition of your own death and do not expect to live until spring, she can take pity. If you are lucky, she may even let you do things with her on the first night for which she might otherwise make you wait a month or longer.

I had listened to the more experienced partisans discussing this tactic and eventually found an opportunity to try it out on Zosia, a pretty nineteen-year-old who was bright and well-spoken. She came from a village close to a vodka distillery we had raided after stopping to rest up for a couple of days. There was a party and each of us received a whole bucket of raw spirit which we mixed with burnt sugar to make it a little easier on the palate. We roasted pigs on spits and there was music and dancing. If I had bedded Zosia, the festivities would have been perfect, but, while friendly and attentive, she did not prove easy.

Perhaps my technique needed polishing or perhaps she just did not like me that much, as she said she was not that sort of girl when I began kissing her. I consoled myself with the liquor and woke up the next day slumped against the wall of a pigsty instead of lying in her arms. She had gone off with one of the NCOs, a cavalry sergeant from pre-war times who performed tricks for her on his horse and played her songs on a guitar.

They disappeared into the night long before I keeled over and went to sleep next to the pigs. As my superior, her conqueror was always telling me I was the youngest and so had to do my stint of guard duty first, no matter how hard I complained.

'You're a good soldier', was his reply, even when I had not slept for two days and nights. I could not compete with him for a woman, and anyway Zosia made her own choice.

A month later we approached the village where I had recovered from the accident to witness a group of Wehrmacht soldiers rounding up the few inhabitants for a forced labour brigade. Some 40 Germans had arrived in half-empty personnel carriers which they intended to fill with able-bodied adults of both sexes from the scattered woodland communities. Although we outnumbered them three or four to one, we still sensed that they very probably had reinforcements near at hand. They had not seen us when we took up positions and the word passed along the line, 'Wait for the order. Direct fire at the soldiers, mind the civilians.'

When the shooting started, the Germans ran for cover, some fleeing back along the track to the next village, others returning our fire. We had opened up with rifles and killed half a dozen of them for the loss of two men and a few wounded on our side. But soon the Germans had scarpered down the track, taking most of their civilian captives with them, as we had not had time to cut off their escape route.

Zosia's sergeant turned out to be the worst hit: a bullet had ripped open his intestines, entering his left side to emerge from the front of his stomach, which disintegrated into a gaping mess of blood mixed with guts and excrement. He stank in his agony. We bundled him and two others onto stretchers and charged back into the forest, clambering down the ravine which ran round the settlement and then fighting our way through the undergrowth at a fast trot, fearing, rightly as it soon turned out, that the Germans would return with artillery, mortars and reinforcements. Weighed down by the stretchers, we halted for a brief rest and to let a paramedic tend the sergeant's wound. He lay doubled up on the stretcher I had helped to carry. The paramedic had no morphine and could do nothing much except stem the flow of blood with cotton swabs dipped in spirit.

We all knew he had a couple of hours to live at most, and by now the Germans had returned in force to the settlement and had started to bombard the forest. Had we not moved when we did, they would have killed many more of us. We took turns on the stretcher as he groaned and screamed at every jolt before stopping for another rest. The paramedic held his hand as he died and promised to look after the little daughter he had left with neighbours.

Zosia raced out to greet me when we got back to her village a fortnight later.

'Where is he? When's he coming?' she asked.

'He's no longer with us. He's gone,' I answered and averted my gaze as she tugged on my sleeve and danced in front of me.

'When will he come back? Where's he gone?'

'Never,' I said and turned to look at her. I sensed that she knew what I was going to say.

'He's dead.'

She cried so much that one of my comrades thought that I had hurt her and told me that I ought to be ashamed of myself for hitting a Polish woman.

After two days on the march without sleep or proper rest, I was put on first watch at the edge of a village. I crawled inside a large conifer to find myself in a tent formed by the lower branches where it was large enough for me to stand upright and peep out at the road leading to the village. Anybody entering the village would have to pass by the tree, which made it the perfect hidden look-out post. But I was dropping from tiredness, dying to sleep, and I could not keep my exhausted eyes open. I fought with my body to stay awake, stood up and stretched and then jumped up and down on the inviting bed of pine needles, untouched by the snow which lay thick everywhere else. I shook my head, rubbed my eyes and slapped my face, but the exhaustion gradually overwhelmed me. Again and again I caught myself falling into a semi-conscious trance, a state of half-waking, half-sleeping during which I was vaguely aware of the noises about me which mixed with my erratic dreams.

It was not a proper sleep because of my fear of being found at my post with my eyes shut, and when towards dawn the roar of engines grew steadily louder, my conscious mind knew that the sounds were real and I imagined a convoy of German troops preparing to attack the sleeping unit. My unconscious mind refused to respond: however hard I struggled to rouse my body to raise the alarm, my eyes stayed closed and my limbs motionless. My body, like a half-dead soldier, rebelled against my commands, but the noises got louder by the second. Then came some shots, after the second guard positioned towards the middle of the village had fired at them. The rest of the unit jumped out from the houses and barns where they had slept and opened up on the unsuspecting Germans, who had obviously stumbled across our position by accident. The vehicles turned out not to be tanks, as I had at first supposed, but armoured personnel carriers.

They retreated at greater speed than they had come, firing from the rear of their vehicles and evidently not ready for a fight against an unknown number of partisans. Now more or less awake, I watched them disappear, passing thirty yards from where I stood. I probably could have shot a couple of our attackers, but they would have got me for sure and so I kept perfectly still. Nobody had been killed on our side and in the general chaos of an early-morning surprise nobody questioned my failure. Everyone was tired, including the CO, and I don't think he realised who in the end had raised the alarm. If there had been more Germans, or if they had been after us, my sleeping could have resulted in heavy casualties. We moved into the forest now that they knew where we were and would certainly return to get us.

The plaque put up by the post-war Communist regime to commemorate the Poles who died in the Puszcza Solska puts the figure at 2,000. We were not the only partisans operating from there in the early spring of 1944: there were Soviets and

Home Army battalions, trapped like us when four or five divisions of Kalmuks, some 50,000 troops, backed by German forces surrounded the forests. The losses inflicted by the Soviet and Polish units had been increasing through the winter and the reprisals, which had escalated with each blown-up train and ambushed column, had been having little effect.

The Germans occupied all the surrounding villages, sealed off the roads and tracks leading from the forests, dug trenches and fortifications at points where we might break out and even flew aircraft over our positions, which meant we were suddenly unable to make fires in the dread cold of late winter. When the fortifications were complete, they sent in the Kalmuks either to destroy us on the spot or to flush us out for their waiting troops to finish us off in the open. We always heard the Kalmuks' progress as they whooped and hollered, both to scare us and to banish their own fear. As we could hear them coming, we were sometimes able to mount an ambush in a clearing.

Everyone in the unit knew the terrain by now and we had experienced local men who knew it even better, whereas the Kalmuks did not. Their strategy was nevertheless well worked out and perilously effective, their numbers eventually overwhelming. They took control of the forest section by section, making us retreat ever further and at an ever more frantic pace. We marched for three days and nights with barely a break, first thirty miles in one direction, then twenty in the other, after finding our exits blocked off on each side. By this time they had cut the forest in half.

Not sure what to do, we tailed two companies of Soviets led by a young major who wanted us to join him in a break-out attempt. At one point the forest made a finger less than half a mile wide and he thought he could force his way through the tip by sending in waves of men, the typical Soviet tactic. As there seemed to be no strategic advantage in our joining forces, we held back, waiting to see how he fared and hoping to slip through after him. The Soviets had 1,000 more men in reserve anyway, and far more firepower than us.

The major cried '*Pirod!* Forward! Attack!' but within half an hour they were scurrying to retreat. It was an entirely pre-dictable massacre: the Kalmuks opened fire from both sides, night became day as flares rained down and guns fired from all directions, the staccato of the machine guns overlain by the whoom-whoom of the artillery. The lives of their own men were always cheap to the Soviets but the major was killed along with half his company. The wounded were left where they lay and a staff sergeant took command. By this time we all knew well and truly what we were up against and that the days of hit-and-run attacks were over.

We traipsed back in the direction we had come, our numbers reduced by at least a tenth and our morale at a low ebb. It was wet and cold, though not snowing, but we had nothing to eat except for a few sacks of sugar, left over from a raid on a depot a few weeks earlier, and ersatz coffee made from burnt barley and chicory. The Kalmuks were now rampaging through every stretch of the forests, screaming like lunatics, chasing us from place to place and denying us rest. That sense of unreality which had overwhelmed me when I thought I was dead in Laskuv hit me again. I fought my fear as it crept over me with the conviction that I had already died in Laskuv and that there was nothing more they could do to me. The logic of the situa-tion dictated that there was no escape and that we were done for, but I repeated to myself a military saying I had overheard at the base in Kremenets many years before, 'An honourable death is better than a dishonourable life.'

Then came the wailing noises, the battle cries of the Kalmuks interspersed with the explosions of hand-grenades and machine-gun fire. They had caught us as we slept. I jumped to my feet when I heard the sounds, but suddenly found I could no longer control my fear, made worse by tiredness, hunger and cold, and my body refused once more to do what I wanted. I was unable to move but my limbs shook as the bullets flew in all directions. In fifteen seconds it was all over and I had finally taken cover without firing a shot. The survivors from our side now stood their ground as the Kalmuks ran off. I have no idea how many bodies were scattered, as there was no opportunity to count and the others stripped the enemy dead for food before I could.

We now found ourselves in complete disarray, exhausted, hungry and afraid, our discipline all but disintegrated as we trudged onwards with no clear command and no formation. Stragglers who were unable to keep up fell back and became lost in the darkness.

As dawn was breaking, voices called out in Polish, 'Here! We're over here! Help! Come quickly!' and we ran through the oval-shaped clearing to join them, thinking that we would get food or that the CO was with them, that maybe they even knew how to get out of the forest. Three-quarters of the way across, the sky ignited. They opened up with mortars, machine guns, grenades and anything else they happened to have. Every tenth bullet was a tracer, which lit up the sky like a thousand shooting stars. I dived beneath an enormous tree trunk and found myself crunched next to someone pushing me from the side, anxious like me to protect his body from the explosions. When the hand-grenade that was meant for us both burst in front of the trunk, my right shoulder took part of the force of the blast. The other fellow seemed more badly injured, but I had no time to notice whether I had picked up as much as a scratch, as the adrenalin pumping through my veins dispelled the pain.

Jackal lay flat out in front of me, blasting back at the Kalmuks with a machine gun. Even after hits to his hip and his left arm, he still carried on firing until his magazine was empty. He then crawled with one leg and one arm to the edge of the clearing and tumbled down a bank into a stream, where he was found, still breathing, three days later.

I ran for my life through the slimy undergrowth in the semi-darkness, my head down, eyes rooted to the ground, until I fell with a great pain in my head, convinced I had been hit and that my life was over. I put my hand to where my head hurt and felt wetness which I took to be blood. 'My skull must be smashed,' I thought, but I still had no idea my shoulder had been torn open. When I glimpsed the dark redness on my hand in the early light I thought it must from the head wound. As I lay perfectly still, my shoulder began to ache and I realised that I must have fallen as a result of bumping my head into a tree.

There had been some 200 of us at the clearing and at least half must have perished. The remainder were now hopelessly lost, torn, bloody and demoralised. I learnt years later that most of the survivors from the ambush escaped from the forest with a Home Army unit. They slipped through the perimeter defences by sacrificing a whole company of their own men to create a distraction a few hundred yards away.

By daybreak I was part of a group maybe 40 strong, some of whom I did not even recognise, including a silly corporal who made more fuss than he was worth. My feelings had somehow changed completely after the shock had subsided and I had realised that my head had not been injured and that once more I had not been killed. It was a great surprise to be still alive.

After the group had ambled about aimlessly for half an hour like frightened cattle, I suddenly heard myself take command for the first time in my life.

'Hold it,' said a voice, which was definitely my own. 'We're getting nowhere and we're sitting targets. They'll hit us again before we've even noticed them, just like this morning. We must split up and go forward in formation. You and you,' I gestured to two fellows with a sub-machine gun, 'you take the main track 200 yards ahead of the rest of us and raise your arms if you see anything.'

This was all straight out of the training manual and should have been second nature to soldiers who had been in the field as long as we had, but still I was amazed to hear myself speak the words, announcing calmly that I was now in charge, and even more amazed that everyone moved to obey me. Soldiers are always glad to think somebody else knows what is happening.

'You and you, walk in front but not on the track, go above through the trees, so you can see ahead.'

I positioned another man at the rear and we continued in a more orderly fashion. As we approached a turning, those at the front stopped and gestured to ask which way we should take and I decided we should get off the main track. We took the turning and landed in marshlands where we quickly found ten men and a paramedic from my original unit.

'What took you so long?' they wanted to know. They had been there for several hours and had already encountered Kalmuks wading thigh-deep in the water, which in this way afforded some protection to the defenders. Among them were two sergeants and so I relinquished the command as quickly as I had taken it. We waded in single file through the water to a hump of raised ground where we thought we would be safer. On the way we came across a cow standing up to its knees in water, and we tugged and goaded it to follow us. Most of us had eaten nothing for six days and the thought of food, even raw meat torn off a fresh carcass, took our minds off any other danger. Polecat had once shown me how to kill a cow by hammering it on the head with an axe and then hacking off its flesh. The trouble was that we had no axe and could not shoot it because that could have given our position away, so we fastened bayonets, balanced the animal on the dry land and tried, without having much room to manoeuvre, to shove a blade into its heart. Unfortunately our bayonets were blunt, as we never sharpened them, and not even a drop of blood issued from its skin as it struggled to free itself. Somehow no one could hit it over the head properly either and the cow survived and then disappeared into the water.

The next day a party of Kalmuks passed by, edging their way forward in single file, up to their hips in the freezing water. We hid by immersing ourselves behind any available bush, arranging chunks of moss over our heads. They took twenty minutes to pass us and we staggered back onto the land. Now we were sodden as well as cold and hungry and there was no chance of lighting a fire because the smoke would give us away. We had no shelter and the second night was worse than the first. Without speaking a word, a paramedic sidled up to me on the ground and hugged me to her, wrapped her legs round mine and pushed and pulled my body so that it covered her, rubbing her hands on my chest and dragging my hands through her hair. In this way we shared what was left of our body heat and the night passed.

It was mid-April and the weather was nothing like as severe as it had been. That saved us. On the third day another line of Kalmuks missed us by a good quarter of a mile. Then a different group took us by surprise. As they approached our position, we watched their anxious progress, their eyes peering in all directions, their ears pricked for every sound. Perhaps they had heard a noise because we had plunged into the water very hastily. Then someone panicked and leapt onto the hump of land and they mowed him down in an instant as the rest of us began to fire and lob grenades back at them. Unfortunately grenades are useless if they explode after impact with the water's surface, as the force of the blast is taken by the water. A corporal yelled the order to count to three before throwing them so that they exploded in mid-flight or directly they hit the surface. The Kalmuks took to their heels, but not before we had hit several of them and they had killed a quarter of our men. The water was now strewn with bodies and equipment, but that day I did at least manage to get some lunch, some half-eaten bread that was stained with blood, concentrated peas and a tin of meat which I found in a Kalmuk's pouch.

Now they knew the location of our hide-out we had to move quickly. That evening we found Jackal on a stretcher with half a dozen others from the unit. He had survived his wound because he had been able to drink, as he lay with his head next to a stream, but his hip was crawling with maggots and it looked to me as if it would do for him sooner rather than later. I watched as a paramedic, who still carried the rudiments of a Red Cross kit with her, cleaned his wound out with a stick of cotton wool bathed in iodine. She poked the stick right through the wound three times, on each occasion replacing the cotton wool, so that it came out the other side of his back, as he groaned through gritted teeth. We were on dry land now and hunted about for food, but there was none to be had, not even leaves. All we could do was wait in case a larger and better organised band of survivors chanced to find us.

I leaned against a tree waiting for something to happen and as I stood up again my head spun, my eyes saw blankness and I had to grab hold of the tree to stop myself from falling. I thought that this must be the result of extreme hunger because, apart from the remains of the Kalmuk's lunch, I had eaten nothing for more than a week and it struck me that death from starvation must be long, slow and painful and that I might as well find a quicker route out of this misery. No one moved when I told them I preferred to be shot rather than die this way and so I set off alone to find a road to lead me to a settlement where I would chance my luck.

After three hours or so I came to Jozefow, a large village which I approached cautiously. I spotted an old man who looked as if he was preparing to plough his fields, even though this was the wrong time of year for ploughing. I asked him if he had food and whether the Germans were still there.

'They've gone.'

'When?'

'Last night after dark,' he mumbled.

It was foolish to believe him because he was a simpleton and I had covered only 50 yards to the nearest building, a barn of some sort, when half a dozen Kalmuks jumped out from either side, pointing Russian tommy guns at me.

'*Ruky vierch! Hände hoch!* Hands up!'

They need not have worried as I did not hesitate and my rifle slipped from my good shoulder. I was a messy sight to behold, even for those who had seen a few things. I was barefoot after losing my boots in the marshes, I had no coat, my trousers were torn to the knees and my clothes hung from me like rags. My legs were bleeding, infected and covered with scabs, the bandages on my shoulder were old and dirty. They could have shot me on the spot, but they took me inside for interrogation, beaming with joy after I had unthinkingly answered their questions in Russian, which I spoke much better than them.

There was evidently a special treatment reserved for Russian partisans and they relished the prospect.

'Where do you come from?'

I gave the name of the tiny hamlet where I had convalesced and where the sergeant had his stomach blown open. This answer was met with disbelief.

'Where are your father and mother?'

'Still there, I hope, unless the partisans have got them.' By this time I had cottoned on that they were more anti-Russian than anti-Polish: my brain had suddenly started to function again.

'Are you hungry? We can see you're hungry.'

They gave me a piece of bread and dripping and a glass of milk, which tasted like a feast.

'If you tell us the truth you can have more.'

The questioner now passed me a German-issue cigarette which was filled with a rough, pungent tobacco which made my head begin to spin for the second time that day.

My story was that the Soviets had attacked our village and robbed us of everything we had – food, seed corn and animal feed – and ordered us to harness the horses and load everything onto carts. They had ordered me to drive a cart and threatened my parents and me with machine guns.

'What did the guns look like?'

'Same as yours.'

'Where did you get your rifle?'

'They gave it to me with the ammunition when we had got further into the forests. They had 100 men and ten carts and told me to keep a look-out and that I should fight with them.'

'And what happened then? Why did they let you go?'

'There was shooting and I saw a chance to escape, but I left my father's horses which he had told me to look after. I'm afraid to go back now.'

They called a Polish colleague over to continue the questioning in Polish as they did not believe a Polish peasant boy could speak Russian, even though I had explained that I had gone to school in the east. The Pole now fired the same questions at me, wanting me to repeat everything I had just said, which he had learnt from them, and tested me by speaking quickly. My story stood up the second time and at least the

Kalmuks seemed to accept that I was a Pole. My interrogator then got out a map and asked me the names of villages on the perimeter of the Puszcza Solska. I got them right.

'Why did you keep the rifle?'

'Because I was afraid and I wanted to hand it to the authorities. I'm a working boy and did what my father told me, except I lost his horses. I don't want to get into trouble. I wandered through the forests and haven't had any food for a week. They found me when I came looking for food.'

After an hour or so one of them picked up a field telephone while I remained in front of the interrogating panel. I had a feeling that they had begun to lose interest in me. I understood the word '*schiessen*' (shoot) and realised that he was asking a German superior for orders. When a few minutes later the German, a stooped middle-aged NCO with an unmilitary air who looked more like a schoolmaster than a Wehrmacht sergeant, walked through the door, there was a lively argument in German. I understood '*perfekt russische Sprache*' and '*keine Angst*', punctuated repeatedly with '*schiessen*'.

I was convinced they wanted to shoot me because they were suspicious on account of my ability to speak Russian, even though the rest of my story sounded plausible. One Kalmuk grew particularly excited and I think he explained to the NCO that I spoke Russian better than he did, which was not surprising since it was not his native language. He picked up a rifle and pointed it at me, shouting, '*Warum?* Why?' but the NCO raised his hand and said, '*Nein.*' He tied my hands behind my back with the silver strips used for epaulettes and signalled for me to march in front of him as he pushed his bicycle. He had a Luger in a holster at his side. He has saved me, I thought to myself, but where is he taking me? Should I try to get away? There was a little play in the twine, enough for me to wriggle my hands, as I had the presence of mind to keep them bulged as he tied, but I could not work them free.

I was not unduly frightened since he was not from the SS but a kindly NCO and he had stopped them from shooting me a moment before, but I had never been to Jozefow and had no idea where we were heading. We turned a corner to see an expanse of scrubland which seemed to indicate the end of the village. Then I began to be afraid and thought, 'This is where he is going to bump me off,' as there seemed to be no other reason for his actions. I decided to run, thinking I could go faster than him barefoot and that it would take him a while to get out his gun and shoot. The only problem was the twine round my hands which would not come loose, even after I had tugged half a hand through. If I pulled hard enough all that would happen was that my skin would rip off and I could run. That would be painful, but skin grows back, I reasoned, while a head does not. I looked back at him and he waved to me to move forwards so I quickened my pace and got ten yards in front before he shouted, '*Langsam, langsam!* Slow down!' There was something in his voice which reassured me and I sensed that he pitied me in my grimy, blood-stained state.

At the top of the hill a larger settlement came into view and I realised that we had not left the village after all and that this was where he was taking me. I had apparently escaped death once more. On the other side of the village I saw a compound surrounded by barbed wire, which was obviously where we were headed. There were no barracks and the wire looked temporary but there was a machine-gun nest in one corner. The camp was crowded with hungry, dejected-looking men.

I was kept there for a couple of days with about 400 other Poles, one or two of whom I recognised. People who had been outside the forests told me how the encirclement of the Puszcza Solska had been organised. One had watched as the slave workers dug the trenches and fortifications before getting into wagons which would take them to the Reich. Others, who carried no luggage with them, had got on different wagons: that meant only one thing – concentration camp – which was presumably where they were now going to send us. Now the fortifications were being dismantled, the troops dispersing, their job done and the partisans destroyed in that part of the Puszcza Solska. Further south-east the fighting raged for another month, the partisans helped by Soviet air drops of vital supplies. No one would believe how I had escaped being shot. The death penalty applied to anyone found with a gun or as much as a single round of ammunition.

On the third day they marched us to the railway station, loaded us onto cattle trucks, 60 or 80 men in each, with no windows, no room to sit or lie down, no food, no water, no sanitation and no idea where we were going or how long it would take.

6

Majdanek, April–July 1944

Majdanek is five miles from the centre of Lublin, so close that a railway was never built all the way to the camp and new arrivals, 'the transports', were either marched from the station or driven in lorries. Mostly they walked. In area it was the biggest camp after Auschwitz-Birkenau and as many as 360,000 men, women and children of all ages and nationalities are estimated to have perished there between 1942 and 22 July 1944, when the Germans withdrew. Some who survived that date died shortly afterwards while others were marched to other camps further west to be killed there.

Like everyone else in the region, I knew exactly what Majdanek was and where it was before I arrived there. I had known people who had disappeared there and I had seen trains transporting prisoners to the camp. I had occasionally seen ex-prisoners who had been released to die, stumbling about in the street like zombies, still in their striped pyjamas.

After more wagons were added on the second or third day of our journey, there were at least 2,000 of us crammed onto the train. Some, but not many, of the prisoners in my wagon died, and sometimes I heard shots, which I assumed were directed at would-be escapees, as my own first thoughts were of escape. In fact, the idea of escaping rarely left me once inside the camp. Yet I soon realised that flight was impossible during the two or three brief stops each day when guards passed bread and water inside or let us out to relieve ourselves. They then gave an order for the inside of the wagon, which stank of illness, death and excrement, to be cleaned, although they provided no equipment for us to do this. I remember the spruce trees which lined the track at these stops and the phalanx of guards who stood in front of them. But beyond these few details I have little idea of the country we travelled through and cannot say for sure how we reached the camp. After a while I stopped peeping through the tiny cracks trying to identify the stations we passed. In the middle of the second or third night voices whispered that we had stopped at Treblinka, an extermination camp for the Warsaw Jews, to the north-east of the capital. Whether it was Treblinka or not, we started to move again after a few hours of waiting.

From Lublin station we were marched to the main gates of Majdanek, which led directly into the area for new arrivals outside the compounds. There we were undressed, shorn of all our hair, including hair on the arms and chest and pubic hair, deloused with DDT powder, which was sprayed into every bodily crevice and orifice except the face, in a ritual which was to grow all too familiar, showered and then clothed in striped concentration-camp pyjamas and wooden clogs. As in most camps (Auschwitz and Belsen were the two exceptions), the prisoner's number, which constituted the sole remaining mark of individuality, was sewn onto the tunic rather than tattooed on the arm.

Once our names and numbers had been carefully noted by trusties, prisoners with special jobs within the camp organisation, other trusties doled out the daily ration of food. On a good day, when the bread contained less sawdust and there was a bowl of cabbage and potato soup, the rations may have had as many as 600 calories, less than a half what an adult requires to survive. The amount they gave us was calculated to make each prisoner gradually waste away over a period of several weeks or a couple of months, as only the trusties and others in special occupations got double rations or maybe more. Yet to someone, like me, who had eaten so little for such a long time – not since my capture by the Kalmuks had I had any sort of a meal – this constituted a veritable feast. There was a four-ounce piece of dry, glutinous bread made of flour supplemented with sawdust and potato peelings and which tasted of clay, a tiny cube of coal-based margarine tasting of motor oil, a small piece of salami, a mug of ersatz coffee, which was made from a sort of chicory, and two cigarettes containing a fibre which was certainly not tobacco. Some idiots swapped items of food for extra cigarettes. I devoured everything and so one of my first memories of arriving in the camp was that I had what I considered to be a good meal.

In the main, of course, we received far less food than was officially intended, because once the two or three chefs, whose positions gave them power over thousands, the two dozen cookhouse workers, the deliverers of the ingredients and then the distributors of the food had all filched their extra portions, there was very little left for the great majority of prisoners. I never saw a bone or noticed the faintest taste of meat or fat in the soup. Yet like all the others who survived, I learnt to savour every last mouthful and make it go round and round my gums until it had quite dissolved. That was the way everything was eaten in the camp and that way I could sometimes feel I had eaten a meal.

Some prisoners, personal servants or assistants to the Nazis such as barbers, and craftsmen needed for general maintenance work or the silversmiths who smelted down the tooth fillings of the dead and re-fashioned their jewellery, received more food. These workers were marched by guards into workshops each morning and usually lived in special barracks, separated from the majority. They all received extra rations to keep them alive to carry out their work, as did workers in the hospital laboratory, who usually had some medical knowledge. Life expectancy for the rest of us was two or three months, up to six months in the summer.

I survived Majdanek for two reasons. Firstly, I was in the camp for only a little more than three months, and was very fortunate to arrive after the worst of the winter had passed. Secondly, at a critical point when I felt my body and mind begin to give up the struggle to live, I worked for ten days in the cookhouse. There

Majdanek

I gnawed all day on raw potatoes and cabbage leaves and returned sufficiently strengthened in body, and consequently in spirit, to see out the next few weeks. No one except those with camp jobs survived a winter in Majdanek. I also received extra food for wheeling bodies to the crematoria on days preceding the next transport when room had to be made in the barracks for new arrivals. I did not mind doing this work because of the extra rations which it earned me.

On one occasion I worked in a team cleaning out an empty hut. On the floor lay a few straw mattresses, which a guard told us to salvage along with the wooden bunks which they evidently also wanted to use again. I entered from the bright sunlight outside and blinked for several moments as my eyes accustomed themselves to the relative darkness inside. Even then I had to blink again to grasp that there was a thick, dark cloud covering the entire floor and reaching up past my knees. On closer inspection it was not completely opaque and looked like millions of dots of multi-coloured dust dancing in the sun's half-rays which penetrated the murky windows. It was silent but seething with activity. Suddenly I realised that the cloud consisted of a mass of black fleas, all of them leaping into the air. The head of the detail, himself a prisoner, threw down a chemical to kill the fleas and afterwards ordered us to wade through the debris several times to retrieve the bunks. We then stripped off outside and were sprayed with DDT and given new pyjamas. I never discovered what had gone on in that hut, how many bodies there had been or long they had lain there.

In addition to the trustie jobs and the skilled and semi-skilled camp occupations, a variety of tasks existed for the unskilled. Sometimes for several days in succession we shifted piles of sand and gravel from one end of the compound to the other, using shovels and wheelbarrows. When we had finished, a guard ordered us to shift it back again. There could be dozens of teams doing this at any one time. On other days we had little or nothing to do. As well as working in the cookhouse and carting corpses to the crematoria, I also helped to clean the shower rooms and prepare the barracks for new arrivals. Only trained chefs or waiters, most of whom were then set to clean out the enormous steel vats and scrub the equipment, were normally taken on for cookhouse duties. As cookhouse workers were always getting caught stealing food, there was a high turnover. I was picked out on roll call one morning because, as a new arrival, I looked young and fit. I spent my few days there scrubbing the vats for the soup.

Guards or *Kapos* body-searched cookhouse workers as they left the kitchens each day. The *Kapos*, however, were usually lax in this duty because they themselves depended on extra food. They generally just felt down the back and front of the body before barking, '*Raus!*' So when I put three or four tiny potatoes into my pocket and then lined up for the search, I felt sure that a *Kapo* would never find them. My luck, which had got me the life-saving job in the first place, must have been running out because on this particular day the *Kapos* had been joined by three Ukrainian guards who had taken over the search without me noticing. When one of them found my potatoes, he raised his baton in a well-practised gesture and brought it down to strike me hard on the shoulder, rather than my head, at which he had aimed. I had ducked just in time and his second blow merely grazed me on the side of the leg as I prepared to sprint away. Before he could even raise his arm for a third strike, I was off into the crowd. A single shot rang out behind me as I raced into a hut and dived out of the open window at the back before finding my own bunk once more. That was the end of my time in the cookhouse, but it had given me new strength and a new lease of life. Indeed, it had saved my life.

When a guard or *Kapo* hit you, the only chance of surviving was to get out of the way of the second blow. A first blow is rarely fatal if you are reasonably fit: it is the second and third blows which do for you. However hard the first one came down, you had to spring to your feet and dart into the crowded compound, as I had done when discovered with the potatoes. As we all looked the same and there were always thousands of prisoners milling about at any one time, it was then as good as impossible for the guard to come after you. This strategy saved my life on at least two occasions. On others, when a guard had taken a dislike to my face or, in the first week or so before I had learnt the rules, I had looked a guard in the eye, something they could never tolerate, they chased me. Survival required constant alertness.

There were six compounds arranged in a line. I was put into the first, reserved primarily for Poles. It contained two rows of barracks, twenty-four in all, twenty of which were numbered and accommodated the prisoners. Of the other four, two housed the kitchens and the shower rooms and two were used for storage. I spent whole days counting the bunks and the occupants, mentally measuring distances and capacities, which is why even today I can still remember some details. The lay-out of the next four compounds was identical, as far as I could make out, and only the last, which contained several large ovens instead of barracks, differed. The barracks too were of a standard size: each had four rows of double bunks, built four beds high. A small sack of straw was provided for use as a pillow and a strip of wood ran down the middle to separate the sleepers. There was no mattress and in all the bunks half the wooden slats had been taken away for use as firewood.

The compound next to mine was reserved for 'politicals' and contained a variety of nationalities, but was far less densely populated than the other compounds. As these prisoners were mostly from western Europe they got more food than us. I spoke to some French, Italians and even some Hungarians. An Italian told me that he was a prisoner of war, which I could not understand because I thought the Italians were on the same side as the Germans.

'*Ich – Kommunist. Hitler, Mussolini – Banditen,*' he explained.

A French political beckoned to me one day to approach the wire fence that separated us and tossed a piece of bread over the fence, across the narrow road which ran between the compounds, and onto the ground on my side. I ran to pick it up when out of nowhere sprang an SS man. He pinned me to the fence at the moment I tried to lift the bread to my mouth, putting his pistol to my head before thinking better of shooting me. Instead, he struck me on the side of the head. I went down, but managed to scramble to my feet before the second and more dangerous blow hit me, and I ran into the crowd of prisoners. He knew that he had lost me and got his revenge by carefully and methodically treading the scrap of bread into the mud with his boot until it became a muddy mush that even a prisoner could not eat.

I felt hate that night, hate for the guard, who had not wanted to waste a bullet on me, and hate for the way he had trodden on the bread and looked around so that I could see his smile as he did so. He did not want the bread, he just wanted to deprive me of it. There is a good side to hating because hate can be a revivifying emotion: if you feel strongly enough, then you want to stay alive rather than capitulate and die, which is what the Germans wanted. The SS man did nothing to the Frenchman, who disappeared with the rest of the French contingent a couple of weeks later.

The third compound was for women of all races, and the fourth and fifth were for Jews, mainly Polish- and Yiddish-speaking, although I heard other languages spoken there. The sixth compound was taken up by the crematoria. The Jewish trusties who worked in the crematoria spoke Yiddish and so understood what the Germans said to one another, unlike the vast majority of other prisoners who spoke no German. They sometimes tried to predict the size of the next transport by the numbers being killed to make way for them. The crematoria were consequently a good place to pick up information. The population of all the compounds changed constantly because of the high death rate and the influx of new transports and as a result I cannot be sure of the numbers. It may be that the segregation was not as strict as it appeared to me. The categories and nationalities of prisoners were clearly marked, however: Jews had either the Star of David or the word *Jude* stitched onto each arm and the front and back of their tunic; Poles had a 'P', Russians an 'R' and so on.

Each compound had a gate giving onto a central corridor, which separated the compounds from the guards' quarters on the other side and the area we knew as the cabbage fields where our food was grown, fertilised with human ashes and fragments of bone which glistened in the rain. New transports would be processed in this corridor, which had numerous shower rooms as well as workshops and other buildings. I was never aware of gas chambers in Majdanek and had not been aware of their use before I was captured. It was only years later that I learnt they were in operation at Majdanek and I would say they must have been either in the central corridor or the sixth compound with the crematoria – I suppose the sixth compound is more likely.

The only route to the outside, apart from that through the main gates, was through the open drains which ran along the back of the barracks to the fence before disappearing under a road beyond the central corridor. If I lay down inside the half pipe, no one could see me from the ground, although I was clearly visible from the guard tower. As there was no way of knowing where the pipe led once it went under the road, I never attempted to crawl along it.

The structure of the day was, at least in theory, as precise as the lay-out of the camp. At the entrance to each barrack hung a notice in German explaining at what time meals were served, when each barrack was due for a shower and delousing and at what time the barracks had to be emptied during the day. Reveille took place at six o'clock, when we were supposed to wash, although no one did so unless a guard or *Kapo* supervised the procedure, when some of us pretended to splash water over our bodies. It was cold, we had no means of drying ourselves and dirt did not matter to us. The Germans, however, always pretended to insist on high standards of hygiene and subjected us to the rituals of showering and delousing at regular intervals. Because of the cold prisoners walked at speed through the long corridor of cold-water jets and emerged shivering at the other end. Nobody wanted to use the rough, greasy soap, not least because guards sometimes claimed it was made from human fat. We all had fleas and lice despite the delousing and our lack of hair.

At 6.30 each morning there was ersatz coffee from the cookhouse, which was always warm, if not hot, and then the roll call in the centre of the compound. The guards did not check us by name or number, or even count us, but they went through the barracks to check no one was lying inside. It was a roll call in name only, but they patrolled in front of each row of men, prodding the infirm to see whether they keeled over and selecting others for 'special duties'. They always needed the able-bodied after a new transport of Jews and, whatever these duties were, they evidently did not want witnesses to survive, as the men never returned. As a rule, even after my stroke of luck in the kitchens, I slouched to make myself seem smaller and weaker. Sometimes when the weather was cold and they needed to make room for new arrivals, they kept us standing on the square for as long as five hours. Usually, however, roll call was over within an hour or so. If the weather was cold or it was sleeting or raining, we heard the first thuds of exhausted bodies hitting the ground after an hour. From then onwards the thuds grew more and more regular and after two hours or so the ground was littered with the corpses of the dead and the half-dead. On one occasion hundreds of prisoners had collapsed and it was then that I joined a team of three others to load the bodies, between six and eight at a time, onto wooden carts and push them to the sixth compound. The bodies weighed very little, but many were still breathing and continued to issue per-ceptible moans as we pushed them past the other compounds to the enormous crematoria. There we lifted up one end of the cart and let them slide into a pit, ready for the crematoria workers, all of whom were prisoners, to hurl them into the ovens. Bubbling fat seeped through the doors and splashed into the ash-pit below, as yellow smoke coiled out of the chim-neys, sometimes filling the whole camp with its stench.

The Nazis needed a steady supply of barbers to crop the hair of new arrivals and to shave the heads and bodies of the others. As a result a disproportionate number of those who survived the extermination camps were hairdressers. I am convinced I recognised one of them, the personal barber to an SS sergeant, on a television documentary 40 years later. He was by then a 70-

year-old Israeli and described his work in Auschwitz, where it is possible he had worked before a transfer to Majdanek or, which seems more likely, after the Germans abandoned our camp, as Auschwitz continued to function for six months after the liberation of Majdanek. The sergeant insisted on a full shave twice or even three times a day and liked to take as long as half an hour over each one. He sat on a chair in the open compound as prisoners watched. The barber, who said on the documentary that his nickname had been Bomba, put his finger to his mouth if a prisoner tried to start a conversation on a controversial topic, such as German troop movements, the advancing Red Army or new arrivals in the camp, as the sergeant understood some Polish. He did not mind talking to us about more innocuous matters and sometimes passed on snippets of valuable information. Once he dropped me a piece of bread when his employer was looking in the other direction. He was well-fed and obviously had special rations. He must have been an excellent barber to have kept his job, as the sergeant was a perfectionist and would rub his face repeatedly during his shave, indicating when a particular spot had been missed.

The sergeant liked music and sometimes arrived in the compound with an accordion or even two or three saxophones, clarinets and mandolins, and then ordered Polish prisoners to play for him. He even shouted in broken Polish that anyone who liked listening to music should gather round and enjoy it. I was moved to whisper to a neighbour that he seemed like a nice man and wondered why and how a decent human being like that had ended up in a job like his.

'Don't kid yourself,' someone told me. 'He's slaughtered more people than you've had dinners. He's just homesick. Haven't you noticed he only likes nostalgic music which reminds him of Germany?'

The racial diversity of the prisoners was matched by that of the guards and *Kapos*. The latter were often German nationals who belonged to the least serious category of prisoner for a concentration camp: common criminals. They were not always bad and sometimes only pretended to beat prisoners because an SS man had come into sight. They carried square batons, like particularly heavy baseball bats, and when in the mood struck out indiscriminately. In addition to the German SS, there were Ukrainian, Latvian and Lithuanian SS guards, most of whom spoke their superiors' language very poorly, but nevertheless attempted to bark their commands in German. Those few who were fluent gained rapid promotion. Like their German colleagues, they had lost all respect for human life and seemed to live only to continue killing. Their greatest delight would be to order a father to hang his son or a daughter to butcher her mother, in full view of the whole compound. Public hangings and executions of other sorts occurred daily. Attendance was compulsory and it was forbidden to turn away. I taught myself to look without actually seeing by staring into the middle distance and not paying attention to the awfulness in front of my eyes.

The most notorious torturer in Majdanek we called the Black Angel because she dressed in black leather and took obvious sexual pleasure from flogging men's genitals and castrating them with her steel-tipped whip. Even the male guards, who treated murder as a sport, winced when she cracked her whip in the direction of a naked prisoner. Her sessions in our compound were intermittent, certainly not daily, as she also operated in the other compounds and in the barracks for new arrivals. If ever she ordered, '*Kommen Sie her,*' the victim either ran or perished painfully. I once saw her select four athletic young men who, from their broad shoulders, were obviously new arrivals. She then ordered the *Kapos* to undress them and tie their hands behind their backs. They stood in a line, their backs to the rest of us, as she aimed the steel tip of her whip at their testicles. Despite her lethal aim she sometimes missed, or through fright the victim's testicles shrivelled completely from view. Then she shot at the man's penis with a pistol, taking care not to kill him, as he collapsed screaming into a pool of blood.

There were rumours of more and worse sexual torture that she practised on fit new arrivals in the central corridor, but I did not witness this. I was not interested in trying to find out which stories were true and which untrue or in discovering where the various screams came from and what caused them. There were so many screams, so many ways of torturing people and so many bodies. I believe the Black Angel was caught and executed after the war.

For guards like her, torture had become a compulsive ritual: it was as if their day would not have been complete without a victim, their job not done without a murder, as if torture had become a way of life for them. They derived their sole pleasure from watching the sub-human races scream in agony. Among these torturers was a sergeant who could be distinguished from his colleagues by a special insignia on his shoulder, which indicated, or so I assumed, membership of an elite, even more brutal, branch of the SS.

Whenever he walked through the compound gates, there was a frenzied movement to the huts, if they were open, or to the far side of the compound, if they were shut. He carried a leather-covered club which must have been filled with lead. He strolled purposefully into the compound every second or third day. Sometimes one victim was enough for him and he departed satisfied; sometimes he needed more. His action with the truncheon was as swift as a panther's: one blow and the man was on the ground with no chance of getting up again. Another blow and the skull was fractured; a third and the man ready to be carted away. He wore white gloves, like many of the SS, and once he had finished with a victim he took out a handkerchief to wipe them, even though his truncheon had done the gruesome work and his gloves had not touched the body. Then he handed the truncheon to a guard, who cleaned it for him, and took out a cigarette, which was lit for him by another guard.

My memory of Majdanek is of unrelieved horror, brutality and fear. So many unspeakable acts were committed each day in front of my eyes that it is odd that one or the other of them should seem so much worse than the rest and that those incidents should have stuck in my memory and invaded my nightmares so often since then. As well as the actions of Black Angel and the special SS sergeant, I have a particularly vivid memory of the death of a young gypsy woman and her baby. I have seen her face so many times in my dreams that whenever I think of what happened to her it seems that I am recalling something which took place only recently.

One afternoon I saw two guards shepherd a crowd of young women through the central corridor to the entrance to the guards' quarters opposite. At the entrance other guards looked at the women's faces, prodded their bodies and lifted up their skirts with sticks before indicating to perhaps every tenth woman to continue into the guards' quarters. I took a broom and pretended to sweep outside my hut in order to have an excuse for approaching the fence. Wafts of perfume and the smell of roasting meat blew across towards me, together with the sounds of men laughing. To get a better view I lay down in the drain and pretended to poke the broom into the pipe as it disappeared under the ground, only 40 yards from where the selected women now stood in a huddle. That way it seemed as if I was working and no one noticed that I was looking at the waiting women.

When a guard signalled for her to come forward, a dark-haired girl in the middle of the group turned, enabling me to see her finely chiselled profile. She had black eyes and long, flowing black hair very much like some of the Jewish girls I had watched bathing in the river from the beach outside Hrubieszow before the war. She held her hands close to her chest and clung to a thick blanket which covered her body down to her ankles, leaving only her face visible. The guard presumably wanted to inspect her figure before sending her inside the barracks to the SS party. Peels of laughter rang out as she resisted when he tugged the blanket from her. They stopped laughing when the baby she had been sheltering beneath the blanket began to cry. She turned towards me, still clutching her child to her breast, and then tried to run. I have seen her do this and heard the baby crying so many times since then. I always wake up at this moment. Fifty years ago, however, I watched for long enough to see her attempt to flee, the guard release his two alsatians and for the dogs to bring her to the ground. Then I turned away. From the screams I have always assumed that the dogs killed both her and her child.

More than the whims of the individual guards, I feared a dull, resigned feeling inside me which I had to fight and fight again in order to keep it from taking over my whole body, crushing my will and destroying my determination to survive. It was that feeling of unreality that had hit me several times after Laskuv. Now it kept recurring. It threatened to invade my body and my mind and made me want to accept anything and every-thing that was going to happen to me, to resign myself to my fate and to give up the life-sustaining hope of surviving. It told me that I was not alive because I had died already in Laskuv: 'Why should you care? You're already dead. What can happen to you? You're not of this world any more. They can't beat you to death because you died in Laskuv in the snow-drift. You were killed in the ambush.'

We called those who succumbed to this condition zombies because when hunger overcomes hope, the victim inches unconsciously over a threshold separating life from death within life. Physical pain disappears and a numbed listlessness takes over. Then nothing matters any more: whether or not you eat, whether or not you survive another day. None of it matters any more. I saw countless men merely going through the motions of living and surviving, not caring whether or not they got their soup, not savouring every mouthful of it and not com-peting for an extra scrap or crust. They had stopped speaking and stopped reacting to their environment; their glazed expres-sions indicated that they had sunk into a personal oblivion which promised release. They had a few days, perhaps a week, to live. A full belly is the only cure, which is why the few days in the cookhouse saved me. Before the cookhouse I had very nearly succumbed to utter depression on a dull, greyish day when the sky hung heavily in the air and yellowish smoke wafted across the whole camp from the sixth compound. There was no breath of wind to disperse it. I lay on my bunk and thought to myself that in a few days' time my body would stink like that foul, smoke-filled air and I prayed to God, for the last time in my life, that he should let me escape from this place before I disappeared into a cloud of smoke. As I prayed, I cried. It was not death that terrified me as much as the thought that my body would stink like the smoke and there would be nothing left of me except that smell. I had lost hope of living and so had no reason to fear death. Yet still I did not want the whole of my being to disintegrate into a small puff of stinking yellow smoke.

This must have been some time in late April or early May and the cookhouse saved me. Hopes of survival were nourished by news of a heavy German defeat towards the end of May. The camp was always rife with rumour. Rumours of fresh killings and new methods of torture and rumours that the Red Army was not far away. Sometimes a guard dropped a newspaper, a German-speaking prisoner overheard a conversation or new arrivals brought news from the outside world. Suddenly the guards, even the Ukrainians, no longer smiled: the news had been bad for them. The non-zombies began to feel that the day might come when we could leave the camp and resume our lives. We knew that none of us could survive a winter in the camp and that rescue had to come before the autumn turned to winter. The death toll was still as high as ever and the bodies of those who died in the night had to be dragged outside to be carried away in the morning. This was a daily ritual, as unremarkable as slopping out in a prison, but the scale of the task the morning following the 'good news' was unprecedented.

My bunk was situated towards the far end of the hut and I usually slept soundly at night, no matter what commotion was going on about me. On this particular night I was suddenly woken by the sound of bullets at about one o'clock. The door at the other end was flung open and several SS had started to spray the barracks and its occupants with tommy guns, firing indiscriminately into the mass of bunks and bodies. I jumped out of bed instinctively to take cover. Anyone capable of rapid movement who had not been hit by the first burst had dived to the lowest bunks or cowered against the wall. Those who survived, about half of us, did so because the bunks sheltered them. After leaping upwards from the peace of a dreamless sleep, I froze to the spot, my hands and arms supporting the weight of my body which hung in mid-air between two bunks. Someone below tugged at my legs for me to drop down, but I was incapable of movement and stared at the gun barrels. Fear, exhaustion and the feeling that I was dead and they could not get me paralysed me. What saved me this time was the wooden upright next to the bunk which stood in a line of uprights stretching to the door. Bodies lay everywhere after the attack, blood covered the bunks and the bodies of the living. The wounded tried to bind their cuts with the pyjamas of the dead.

This pattern of attack was not repeated. Atrocities decreased in the final weeks before liberation and rations became slightly more plentiful. The Nazis feared that a day of reckoning might come for them. After mid-July we could hear artillery fire in the distance. In the afternoon of 20 July the trusties, Jewish and non-Jewish, and the long-term survivors, like barbers and craftsmen from all six compounds, started to file out of the main gate, turning west, not in the direction of Lublin station but across the fields. They were accompanied by guards and *Kapos* on foot and in vehicles of all descriptions. The whole procession took more than three hours to pass, moving at walking pace, four to six men wide. At a guess, I would say that by dusk two days later as many as 20,000 guards, *Kapos* and trusties had departed. That night a stray shell ripped through the roof of one of the barracks, killing many inside. The following day fires burned in the guards' quarters as the Germans carried out box after box of files and destroyed them. The camp had been in existence for three years and up to 400,000 prisoners had passed through it, each of them counted, numbered and documented. There were mountains of papers to be burnt.

By dusk that evening everything had gone quiet: in the end the Germans sneaked away like thieves. Then, on the point of darkness, four guards armed with two Spandau machine guns opened up with long bursts of fire, scattering their bullets in all directions, as those with sufficient strength dashed for cover. They fired for two to three minutes at a time. As they knew this was not an efficient way of killing large numbers and that most of us had time to hide from the bullets, they must have wanted to distract us as they dismantled the guns in the towers and frighten us into staying there once they had gone.

It was 22 July. We had become prisoners without gaolers, as they had left the gates locked and the fences intact. It was now left to us to break out and I still consider my flight from Majdanek to have been an escape. My first thought, however, was of food and my first idea was to break into the storeroom, where I grabbed a loaf of camp bread and a tub of coal margarine. I could not find any salami but gobbled down half a pound of margarine and half a loaf of bread, more than I had eaten in the previous fortnight, barely stopping to chew until my belly could take no more. The meal made me sick for days afterwards, but for the moment I had no time to think of my stomach. Thus fortified, my next objective was the compound gate and the route to the outside. Several prisoners levered open the gate with crowbars, but, instead of charging outside towards life and the future and away from this factory of death, as was my intention, they merely stood there and gazed across the fields.

'Let's go. Who's coming with me?' I asked. 'There's nothing to fear. They've all gone.'

It did not bother me that no one wanted to move. They were frightened they would be caught again and shot by the Germans.

I believe that most of the other survivors were still inside the compound when the Red Army entered two days later.

7

The Road to Freedom

Outside the fence I discovered piles of clothing from one of the last transports. I pulled some trousers and a jacket on over my pyjamas and found some half-decent boots. As I walked away up the hill, I thought to myself that there had been ex-soldiers and policemen in the camp, even ex-officers, but it seemed that none of them had dared to break out into no man's land. No one liberated me from Majdanek: the Germans retreated and I walked out after them. After clambering through the cabbage fields, still ankle-deep in human ashes and fragments of charred bone, I reached the perimeter fence. As no guards were watching, it was easy to crawl under the wire and I disappeared into the woodlands and small fields that stretched towards the outskirts of Lublin. I had terrible stomach ache and diarrhoea all that night as a result of the large quantities of camp food I had eaten, but that did not bother me too much. I was free and I wanted to get back home or, failing that, back to people from my own side.

People with no experience of war often think that a front line is straight and clearly demarcated, but in fact this is rarely so. In eastern Poland in July 1944 the line zigzagged back and forth, and sometimes there were Soviet units twenty miles west of the German rearguard. In between the two vast armies lay no man's land, which is where I now found myself. I knew it was too dangerous to walk on main roads and that it would be crazy to go near Lublin until the battle for the city was over. But by the time I stumbled across a German machine-gun nest the following morning, I had grown used to the rumble of tanks and the thud of artillery firing in the distance. The Germans might have been in full retreat – in little over a week the Red Army would reach the outskirts of Warsaw – but the Wehrmacht remained disciplined to the last and stuck to its task of slowing down the Soviet advance and disrupting advance units of Cossacks.

Two women spotted me moving across the fields and cautiously approached me. They turned out to be Polish and I was convinced that I had seen the older one, who wore a beret, in Hrubieszow earlier in the war. We all three slept in a barn that night and spent the next two or three days together, waiting for the fighting to subside. The woman in the beret told me I needed to eat sugar or honey dissolved in water and mixed with bread in order to calm my stomach and give me energy. Well-intentioned as her advice undoubtedly was, I found it pretty useless as none of these things was available, although I still had some camp bread, which was good enough for me to eat. Her attention reassured me, though, and I repaid them for their company by explaining the different sounds made by the mortars and machine guns we heard during the night. It was nice to be in female company again and I enjoyed talking to the two young women.

In the day we wandered about rather aimlessly, avoiding explosions, until we reached a village where one of the women had a cousin who would give us food. On seeing how terribly skinny I was, her family wanted to feed me a bowl of smetana, but the woman with the beret said that it would do me no good and that I should have bread mashed in sweet water, as she had prescribed before. They did not know why I was so underfed and I did not tell them, nor show them my ribs poking out beneath my jacket. After a couple of hours I went back into the village, which had been unscathed by the fighting, to see a crowd of peasant women as they were leaving church. It was a Sunday, I realised. Then came the familiar sound of machine-gun fire followed by the sight of about 80 Cossacks on horseback shepherding a dozen German prisoners, some of whom lay on stretchers carried by their fitter comrades.

What surprised me now was that the village women brought out food for the soldiers on both sides and even tried to minister to the German wounded. A young Pole had different ideas and screamed for someone to fetch him a gun so that he could finish off the German bastards. I too would have shot them without a moment's hesitation if anyone had handed me a weapon and told me to get on with it, although I was so worn out that I found it hard to feel either hatred or pity. I lacked the energy to feel jubilant at seeing my tormentors on the run or enjoy their undergoing much the same treatment that we had suffered at their hands for so long. None the less it amazed me that these Polish church-goers could feel so much compassion for German soldiers. Several of them rebuked their young compatriot and screamed that he was a godless animal for wishing to kill a defenceless human being. A couple even started to pray for him.

One of the Germans, emboldened by this display of forgiveness, now began to address the assembled crowd. To my astonishment, his Polish proved flawless. He told them he came from Silesia, a predominantly German-speaking region which fell to Poland after the war.

'Only my mother was from a half-German family. My father was a true Pole. I am a Pole. They made me join the army when I was seventeen.'

'You'll be all right,' one of the women assured him. 'They won't kill you'.

Two more of the unwounded prisoners turned out not to be Germans either. Like several of the Cossacks, including the captain, they had Kalmuk features. But this pair were renegades, like the Kalmuks we had fought in the forests. Speaking to them in Russian, the captain asked them their names and where they came from, and after this brief interrogation he turned in true revolutionary style to his troops to ask their advice.

'These two men, formerly citizens of the Soviet Union and soldiers in the Red Army, have borne arms against us. They have fought against socialism on the side of the Nazis. They are wearing German uniforms. Do we need further evidence? There is proof enough that they are traitors – and there is only one law for traitors.'

His men all nodded in agreement and he ordered a corporal to take the pair outside the village and have them dig a hole.

'You know what to do.'

We heard the salvo a few minutes later.

A Cossack NCO asked me where I came from and I lifted my jacket to show him my concentration camp pyjamas and my skinny body.

'We've seen worse than you,' he said. 'You'll be all right now. You are liberated.'

Two days later I approached Lublin along the Warsaw Road, which had once been a magnificent avenue lined on either side with plane trees and parkland, dotted with imposing public buildings and the houses of the wealthy. A military hospital stood in the middle of one of these parks and that was where I headed. On the way I passed three charred Soviet tanks with their turrets blown away. The stench of rotting flesh in the July heat was intense. They were from the Ukrainian front under Rokossovsky and had been knocked out by artillery from the Byelorussian front under Koniev, who had converged on Lublin from the north-east, ignorant that his Ukrainian comrades had already reached the city from the south-east. Some houses had been peppered with bullets and here and there I could see evidence of mortar shells, but there was very little structural damage and no evidence of bombing. The Germans had retreated without putting up a fight, but the city was still in turmoil and the survivors had no desire to celebrate their liberation, however great their relief that the Germans had gone.

I made my way to the military hospital, which had quickly switched from nursing German casualties to treating the Soviet wounded. Many of the nurses had been Polish all along; only the staff doctors, German personnel and Wehrmacht patients had been evacuated. The buildings stood 200 yards from the

Warsaw Road, surrounded by trees and greenery. Patients in wheelchairs sat outside to soak up the sun's healing rays.

I told a nurse that I could not take food because it ran straight through me and gave me terrible pains, but she just said that this was a military hospital and could only take army personnel, not civilians, and that I should go somewhere in the city where I would be looked after. I found the Polish Red Cross hospital in the centre of Lublin. It had kept going throughout the war and now had space for me in one of its crowded wards. Even though the Germans had taken most of the movable equipment, the doctor was able to give me an X-ray, while a nurse washed my filthy body and applied cream to kill the various parasites which infested me. She dressed me in clean cotton pyjamas which smelt of fresh laundry. The staff all showed sympathy, but patients like me were a common sight.

They started me on easily digested special biscuits packed with protein which they fed me every hour with a glass of sweet water. After two days I went onto a starchy, milky concoction, and then two days after that was allowed chicken soup with noodles and potatoes mashed in gruel, all of which was still in very short supply. The ward was on the fifth floor and every inch of space was filled with the wounded and the half-starved. A man next to me refused to go near the window because he said all windows made him want to jump, but he would peer from a distance of a few yards and ask me what I could see. Soviet troops crowded the streets and I glimpsed a truck with the words 'Berling Army', the name of the Polish forces under Soviet command.

'You're lucky,' he said to me, 'if you can look through a window.'

He then explained that the Gestapo had tortured him on the top floor of their headquarters and regularly taken him to the window and threatened to throw him out. Once they had suspended him by his feet and he had thought they were going to drop him. I liked him and felt I could talk to him because of what we had both gone through.

After two weeks I had made a reasonable recovery and had

put on enough weight to be discharged. I went straight to the Soviet recruiting centre where thousands of Poles, eager to continue the fight against the Germans, lined up to be admitted into the army, the air force or even the navy. We could not think of peace and I did not consider trying to trace my family until later. The food was good and we slept in barracks in the city, waiting for a full vetting. For me this meant that after all I had been through, my boyhood dream of joining the air force might finally come true. There was, however, one difficulty: the humbler your family origins, the greater your chance of acceptance. Since the working class and peasantry were to form the bedrock of the new Communist state in the process of being formed in the liberated territories of Poland, my family connections, especially on my father's side, did not count in my favour.

When I was directed into the prefabricated building to be interviewed by an officer from the Soviet security police, the dreaded NKVD, forerunners of the KGB, I knew I had to lie.

'Where is your father?' was the first question.

I was telling the truth when I said that I had no idea where he or the rest of my family were living or, indeed, whether they had survived the German occupation.

'What is your father's profession?'

'He works in a flour mill.'

That sounded promising to my interrogator, but he still wanted me to specify what he actually did in the mill. I replied that he unloaded sacks of grain, which, in a few years' time, would turn out to be strangely prophetic.

'And how is it that you speak such good Russian?'

'My family moved to the western Ukraine when I was young so that my father could find work. I learnt the language from Russians who lived there.'

'And when did you join the partisans?'

'Two years ago.'

'How many Nazis have you killed?'

I boasted that I did not know the number, and he then asked me all sorts of questions about where I had fought. My answers seemed to satisfy him.

'What is the most democratic country in the world?'

That was easy.

'The Soviet Union, of course.'

He continued with some questions about the Russian Revolution, on which I scored badly. To my surprise he then offered me a cigarette. Instead of roll-ups made from newspaper, which Russian troops normally smoked, he had long filter-tips, three-quarters cardboard filter and one-quarter tobacco. The cigarette lasted a couple of puffs.

'Why do you want to joint the air force?' he asked in a friendlier tone. I replied that the air force offered a more effective way of killing Germans: rather than pick them off one at a time, as I had done as a partisan, an aircraft could strafe their positions and bomb their cities. He then passed me on to an air force officer who asked me some questions about algebra and trigonometry, which I found easy. I could not answer the physics problem, but he said I was young and would pick the subject up quickly. The same apparently applied to my political education. He told me I would have to pass physical tests before they allowed me to start training and that it would be a while before I could learn to fly fighter planes. I had said I wanted to fly Yaks, forerunners of the famous MiG. I also explained that I was still weak from the three and a half months I had spent in a concentration camp and had not taken any real exercise since my release. He replied that he understood all about that and that I would have time to get fit again. A young man of nineteen was just the sort they were looking for and I felt hopeful for the first time in more than half a year.

We had maps in the barracks which changed every few days as the Red Army marched westwards and prepared to take Warsaw. Next to the maps hung the portraits of each of the Red Army's 40 field marshals. All Poles, however, now wanted to be with the Home Army in Warsaw to take on the Germans in the battle for the city. We had heard eye-witness reports from the wounded sent to recover in Lublin and listened in secret to the news on the BBC. Berling had put his army on red alert and the Soviet radio announced that the heroic people of Warsaw had risen up to fight the Nazis. What they did not mention was that the Red Army had halted outside the city and watched as the Germans put down the rebellion, slaughtering up to a quarter of a million Poles before dynamiting what remained of Poland's capital.

Two days after reporting to the recruiting centre, some time in mid-August, I was assigned to a group of 100 men, most of whom had fought as partisans. Equipped with plenty of light arms, we set off for an aerodrome to the east of Warsaw, not far from Siedlce, which the Soviets evidently intended to put to good use. We were attached to a Soviet unit which was clearing the site of undetonated bombs and other detritus left behind by the Germans. The only explanation for sending us so close to the front was that the Red Army command envisaged crossing the Vistula and moving forward before the autumn. If that was the case, then the course of the Warsaw Uprising must have changed the plan. The Soviets did not keep us here for long and within a week or two I was back in Lublin.

From Siedlce we could hear the German artillery pounding Warsaw into the ground. To our dismay, however, we could not go to the rescue of our compatriots, who were now fighting one of the bloodiest battles of the entire war. Berling was prevented from marching to their aid and suddenly his name disappeared from the newspaper reports. Polish resentment of the Russian liberators can be traced to this date.

My family was amazed to see me when I turned up at Zakzrouvek unannounced at the end of the month, wearing the Polish emblem, shorn of its pre-war crown, a symbol of the aristocracy and bourgeoisie, on my hat. My little brother brought me cherries from the trees we had once climbed together. He told me he had thought I was dead. They had not heard from me for nine months, not since the murder of Kasimir and Anthony in fact, and had no idea where I had been. After everything I had been through, I was surprised to discover that the mill was still working and that the dam had not been so much as damaged in the fighting, which had bypassed the village and our estate. My family even had food to eat.

The Road to Freedom

In late August there was a trial of six war criminals in Lublin. They had been handed over by the Red Army to the Polish Communist authorities whose provisional headquarters were in Lublin. Since Stalin no longer recognised the nationalist Government in Exile, the Lublin Administration, as it came to be known, now claimed to speak for all Poles, both those already 'liberated' by the Red Army and the rest still occupied by the Germans. The Soviets knew that it was important to let the Poles conduct their own trial, which lasted for more than a week, and mete out their own justice. As news of the trial filled the newly established newspapers with details of Majdanek, it was impossible for anyone in the city not to have heard that the commandant and five other SS men had been found guilty of crimes against humanity. Surviving victims had identified them in court.

After one of the accused had committed suicide in his cell, only five men came to be hanged at a spot inside the former camp where they had carried out their crimes. But first they were to be marched from the city centre to the place of execution. While the authorities had counted on the inhabitants lining the streets to watch the condemned men walk to their death, no one could have predicted the numbers who eventually turned out, nor the public fury which threatened to turn the orderly proceedings into a lynching. Official estimates put the crowd at 200,000, which is twice the pre-war population of Lublin. The authorities were barely in a position to control the hatred which they had helped to whip up.

Onlookers hurled flowerpots and cooking pans from their balconies, others spat from the pavements and jostled the military police and Communist militia whose job it was to protect the villains. The atmosphere was frenzied, the power of the crowd awesome as it blocked the road and refused to let the column pass. I joined 300 air cadets to help clear a pathway through the mob. We had been issued with rifles and a few rounds of ammunition, which we were ordered to keep in our pockets and use only to fire over the heads of the protesters if there was a risk of losing the condemned prisoners. In the end we needed the rifles to push past the angry people and open up a corridor for the procession to pass through, then, arms locked together, to hold them back as the condemned men went by. As the crowds were too large to fit into the camp, it was decided to hang the men on some high ground adjacent to it so that as many spectators as possible could watch.

Two lorries were parked next to the gallows where the SS men now stood to hear their sentences read out and receive the last rites. The Poles wanted justice to be done and they wanted it to be seen to be done.

The announcement was read out through a loudhailer. 'For the crimes committed at this concentration camp, not taking into account other crimes which were committed elsewhere, as adjudicated by the highest court of justice in liberated Poland, you are condemned to die by hanging. The priest will give you extreme unction. You may make a last request.'

The commandant was the most repentant and had already broken down in tears, wailing about '*meine Frau und meine Kinder*'. He repeated the defence he had given at the trial that he had been obeying orders and had not killed anyone himself, meaning that he had not actually done so with his own hands. No, I thought to myself, he had worn white gloves when he went out killing, like the other officers. The crescendo of noise from the eager spectators grew more menacing by the second, held back by lines of militia, military police and air force cadets standing in rings three or four men deep.

'Get on with it!' the crowd roared with a single voice.

The loudhailer exhorted them to be patient, but still we could not hold them back and they edged ever closer to the gallows.

'Citizens, comrades, be patient! We are civilised people and a civilised nation. We cannot behave as they did. The priest will hear their confessions and give them the last rites before the executioner performs his task.'

The condemned men already had the nooses placed round their necks, but their heads remained uncovered to the last. The priest now passed along the line and whispered to each man in turn before offering a crucifix for him to kiss. The commandant continued to weep and to beg for mercy. Nobody felt a spark of compassion for him. I could not understand how a torturer who had behaved like a rabid animal could beg in that way. The fourth man was the sergeant who had beaten prisoners to death with his leather-covered baton. I had recognised him instantly. For the first time I now saw him without his hat and noticed his dark complexion and slightly oval, pointed face. He contorted his body forwards to thrust his face and spit at the priest, who jumped backwards as the villain was restrained by guards.

I did not hear what the sergeant said because the noise behind me was so intense, but I read the reports afterwards, which said he had regretted not wiping out the entire Polish population when he had been given the chance. He threatened that if he discovered an evil power beyond the grave, he would return to finish off his work and avenge the indignity he had suffered at the hands of the sub-humans.

The priest moved quickly to the fifth man and dealt with him before stepping down from the makeshift podium. Then the order was given, the lorries moved away and the five bodies kicked and writhed in the air. The sergeant, reluctant to go to meet his diabolic masters, kicked for twice as long as the others and continued to dance in the air after their tongues hung out, white with foam. His strength was unnatural and the spectacle turned the crowd quiet. The pressure from the crowds eased long before he was dead.

Dealing with captured Nazis was not the only item on the Soviet agenda. From the very beginning, indoctrination in socialist ideology was intense at the barracks in Lublin and later, from the beginning of September, at the base in Zamosc which was made into the first military school of aviation in post-war Poland. Political theory lectures took up more than two hours each day and were accorded greater importance than the lectures on aerodynamics, meteorology and aircraft construction, generally considered essential knowledge for trainee pilots. They wanted to drum into the new recruits that the Party was always right, always spoke the truth and could never be contradicted in argument or deflected from its path. Stalin and the Soviet system he had forged in his image were superior to anything the West could offer, for under the Soviet system, no matter how poor you were, no matter how humble your origins, how downtrodden your ancestors, you could redeem yourself and improve your lot through working for the Party and propagating its virtues and the wisdom of Comrade Stalin.

The Party's infallibility was the first article of a new secular faith. We repeated the mantra at regular intervals throughout the day. During the evening recreation period any illiterate moron could exercise his democratic rights by jumping to his feet and declaiming that Comrade Stalin had acted correctly by denouncing such-and-such a practice because the Party had fully endorsed his actions. If the most uncouth peasant, who evidently had not benefited from the most elementary schooling, began such a speech, consisting of barely half a dozen badly memorised sentences, the rest of us were compelled to give him our attention. If someone had fallen asleep on his bunk after fourteen hours' instruction, then his friends shook him awake and urged him to participate in the 'debate'. Needless to say, no genuine debate ever took place because criticism of what had been said could so easily be construed as criticism of the Party or a slight on Comrade Stalin. Men were arrested and taken to labour camps for less. Even officers had to stop in their tracks and listen when someone felt the urge to spout some of this nonsense.

When the speaker had finished, it was as well if others put questions or picked up his thread, which often amounted to little more than repeating his empty phrases. Questions then took a sycophantic form, such as 'How did Comrade Stalin know...?' or 'How did Comrade Stalin acquire this superior wisdom...?'

I was prepared to respect the historical Communists, Marx, Engels and Lenin, because I thought they were idealists who had stuck to their convictions and worked to improve the living conditions of the poor. But when someone who had never read a book in his life and who had just returned from three months' training, freshly promoted to the rank of sergeant (as he lacked the intelligence to become a proper officer), started repeating phrases he had learnt parrot-fashion, then I had no time for it. I just sat back and pretended to listen. I never overcame my mother's snobbishness when it came to submitting to a man of inferior education. Yet it takes effort to battle against a flow of words which gush forth non-stop at all hours of the day, and occasionally I felt myself slipping into passive acceptance of them. I fought to remember that they were telling me lies. I tried to recall the way the Soviet Union had treated Poland in the not-so-distant past.

One old fox, who had been captured by the Soviets in 1939 and fought with the Red Army since 1941, could see I was having trouble learning for the exams. He advised me that the only way to pass was to learn passages by heart and quote them verbatim, no matter what the questioner asked.

'When it comes to the orals,' he went on, 'if you cannot answer the question he is putting to you, start spouting something from Lenin's speeches or repeat a piece of Party doctrine. Switch from the question by saying something like, "The most significant characteristic of the great Democratic Communist Party is the fact that there are people like Lenin and Stalin." Then recite their achievements and their statements to the Party Congress and say what their aims have been and how close we are to fulfilling them. Go on for as long as you like, he has no right to stop you. If you tell him what Stalin has said, then he cannot fail you.'

This was sound advice and I learnt to use it to my advantage.

On Sundays most of the Poles in the squadron at Zamosc filed into church, while I rested on my bunk, revising my lessons or dozing. One morning in October the duty officer entered and, after making a quick inspection of the washrooms, came out and ordered me to fetch a bucket and get cleaning because the latrines were filthy. I replied that I would do no such thing, which took him aback, and he repeated his order rather more loudly. Commissar Schlomin, who as the top Party man at the base was not allowed to attend church, heard the shouting. At his approach I leapt from the bunk and stood to attention. He asked what I thought I was doing disobeying the duty officer.

'I am being punished for following the teachings of the Party. The Party teaches that there is no God and that is why I choose not to go to church. Now I am being forced against Party doctrine to listen to the priests' dogma.'

'No one suggested that you should go to church,' he said.

'No they didn't. Not directly. But if I have to clean the washroom because I am the only one not in church, then next Sunday I will go to church.'

He showed neither anger nor irritation at having lost the argument, and instead a faint smile came to his lips.

'You are free to continue what you were doing.'

Not all confrontations ended so peaceably, however. One morning at reveille I noticed that the fellow in the bunk above mine was missing, which was strange because I had not heard him leave during the night. His bed was made up neatly and looked as if nobody had slept in it. Without thinking, I wondered publicly whether or not he had slipped out without a pass, no doubt to visit a woman in town. Such a comment would normally have been met with a ribald reply.

'Ssh, you idiot,' someone from the next row whispered. Then I tumbled to what must have happened. Nobody mentioned his name again: he had ceased to exist. A dozen or so of my comrades disappeared in this way in the eight months I served in the air force. No one could tell which comrades and colleagues were working with the NKVD, but it was a sure bet that they deployed their spies everywhere.

Pre-flight training was set to last for two and a half months, which seemed far too long to me, but by Christmas I had sat in the cockpit of a UT2 and flown with an instructor. They told me after I had sat in a makeshift flight simulator that my legs were too long to fly a Yak, which had been my ambition because it was the only plane sufficiently light and manoeuvrable to take on the German Messerschmidt. In the New Year they put me in a Stormovik, a fighter-bomber known in the West as the Flying Tank because of its heavily armoured fuselage.

Since the Polish Air Force, which had supplied squadrons of pilots to the RAF during the Battle of Britain and many more to Bomber Command, was still under the command of the Government in Exile in London, we were pioneers of the new democratic flying corps. This new air force needed to build up everything, and most importantly its personnel, from scratch, taking full advantage of Soviet help. Navigators, radio operators, ground staff and mechanics were all needed, not just pilots, and all received their training from Russian experts at Zamosc. At the beginning as many as half the officer cadets were Russian, generally of Polish extraction, although very few spoke Polish with any ease or fluency. Like the Russians with Polish names who filled leading positions throughout the liberated part of Poland, we called them infiltrators, but for the moment we had a common enemy and relations were not hostile. Many of the Poles had been in the Soviet Union since being captured in 1939 and had fought in the Polish divisions of the Red Army. They were hardened pros and had often become convinced Communists. The Soviets knew they could rely on them and reckoned that they would be a good influence on their compatriots who were still unversed in Communist ideology. When the first stage of the training was complete, we divided into a Polish squadron and a Russian squadron: Russians of Polish descent who now wore the Polish uniform were treated as Poles. All they knew for sure about me was what they had been able to check with the Red Cross – that I had been in a concentration camp – and was not likely to be sympathetic to the Nazis.

Tensions between Poles and Russians smouldered beneath the surface and periodically threatened to burst into flame. Leaflets from the Home Army detailing the Soviet betrayal of Poland appeared on the doors of latrines in Lublin, where the locals also risked tuning in to the BBC or Polish broadcasts from abroad. Interpretations of the Home Army behaviour and the disastrous order for the armed insurrection in Warsaw varied.

The official Soviet view was that the Polish aristocracy had exploited the bravery of Polish youth in an attempt to re-establish the pre-war feudal system, but none of us believed that.

A week or two after the Warsaw Uprising had been crushed at the beginning of October, a Russian warrant officer yelled at a young Polish cadet on the parade ground that his rifle was a disgrace. He then called him a 'dirty *Lacki*', an insulting term to any Pole. All the Polish cadets within earshot shared their comrade's sense of offence and held their breath as the cadet hurled his rifle at the feet of the Russian and refused to pick it up again. For a second it looked as if he would strike or even shoot the Russian. Commissar Schlomin, who must have heard the original insult but could not undermine his compatriot's authority by contradicting him directly, now took over. He asked the cadet's name, rank and number and then ordered him to pick up his rifle.

'I'm not picking it up.'

'That's an order. Pick it up.'

The young man's face contorted with anger, defiance and determination. Still he stood upright.

'I will have you court-martialled if you continue to disobey my direct order.'

It was clear that he was troubled at having to bow to the authority of a Russian after the wounding insult. His face had turned red with hate as he looked the commissar in the eye, his fists clenched tightly. Schlomin was tougher, however, and stared the man down. Eventually he jerked to the ground, grabbed the rifle and clutched it to his breast. Once the commissar had crushed the cadet's will, he was satisfied and did not make it a personal matter or rub the cadet's nose in his disgrace. Instead he turned to the rest of us and announced that discipline had to be observed at all times and orders obeyed without question.

'Let this be a lesson to all of you.'

I was impressed at the way he had defused the explosive situation without either inflaming the Polish sense of injustice or undermining the warrant officer.

The Road to Freedom

When Warsaw finally fell in January 1945, Schlomin summoned all ranks to the main hall to announce that the heroic Red Army had liberated the Polish capital. The cheers were spontaneous and the joy genuine, and to celebrate the fraternity of the Polish and Soviet forces he gave us the rest of the day off training. The vodka flowed and the Poles all departed for the town in the evening. My head was still spinning the following morning when I stepped into the cockpit, but the shared victory did nothing to diminish our mistrust of our Soviet 'liberators'.

8

Agent for the NKVD

It was 7 November 1944, the twenty-seventh anniversary of the storming of the Winter Palace, the event which set in train the Bolshevik Revolution. After May Day and New Year, this was the biggest festival in the Communist calendar and we were given three days off to celebrate. I asked the major for leave to visit my family, thinking that his permission would be a formality since most of the others who still had family in the vicinity had already been allowed to go.

To my surprise, he flatly refused.

'You're too lazy,' he said.

'But I've been studying hard, comrade major,' I replied. 'I've done everything that you've required of me in training.'

'Maybe, but outside training you're slovenly. You don't clean up without being asked. You don't keep your bed or your belongings neatly. You don't keep your uniform clean. Your appearance and attitude do not come up to the standards expected of a cadet in the democratic Red Air Force. That's why I'm not letting you go. Let it be a lesson to you.'

'Yes, comrade major,' I answered, still shocked by his response.

I knew there was no point in arguing, but left his office feeling uncertain whether he really meant the criticism or whether it was more a matter of personal dislike. I decided he must have taken against me for some reason and had been waiting for an opportunity to let me know it. This made me furious and I decided to spend the holiday in Hrubieszow come what may.

I slipped out of the base the following evening, hitched a lift in a military lorry and spent a few days with my Aunt Sophie, who was, as ever, pleased to see me. I returned in the early hours of the last day off training, confident that no one would have noticed I had been away, and lay down, exhausted, on my bunk. Indeed, had I arrived back the previous afternoon, nobody would have been aware of my absence. Unfortunately, however, there had been a roll call that evening and I was nowhere to be seen. Schlomin had ordered the base to be searched: when found, I was to report to him immediately. As far as he was concerned, I counted as a deserter, so he must have been surprised to hear that when they found me, I was fast asleep in my bunk. As I followed him into his office, I knew that I was possibly facing a term in Siberia for my disobedience.

He seemed pleased that I had come back, probably because this meant that his hitherto clear desertion record would remain unblemished after all. Once inside his office, he locked the heavy door behind us and, just to remind me that he carried a weapon, flicked his revolver with studied absent-mindedness. He then sat down behind his desk. I stood to attention half-way between him and the door in the middle of the bare room and watched him take a bundle of files out of a drawer and begin to pore over them, reading each line as if for the first time. After several minutes he looked up and stared straight at me without speaking. Then, keeping his gaze fixed on me, he got up, walked slowly in my direction and began to pace around me, still without uttering a sound. My left ear started to itch and I discovered a sudden urge to use the toilet, but I dared not move. After his second or third circuit he spoke very quietly, his mouth pressed so close to my still troublesome left ear that it felt as if his breath blew into my eardrum.

'Do you want to be a pilot, comrade Lotnik?' he asked.

'Yes, comrade lieutenant. More than anything else in the world,' I answered.

'A fighter pilot?'

'Yes, comrade lieutenant.'

'A pilot in the democratic Polish Air Force is a pioneer of a new democratic society. Do you understand that, comrade Lotnik? Has that piece of information yet penetrated your stubborn skull?'

'Yes, comrade lieutenant.'

'A pilot in the democratic Polish Air Force is immensely privileged to be where he is and in return for his privileges he must remember his duties. He has to be completely and utterly reliable, twenty-four hours a day, 365 days a year, because the lives of thousands of his fellow countrymen depend on his actions. He must place loyalty to the Party higher than love for his family and above his devotion to his personal pleasures. These are elementary rules, comrade Lotnik. You have disobeyed them. Do you have anything to say?'

There were quite a few things I wanted to say in my defence, but I knew it was better to say nothing.

'No, comrade lieutenant, I do not.'

'A pilot in the democratic Polish Air Force has to be ready to do whatever the Party requires of him without hesitation and without question,' Schlomin continued. 'That means he has to obey his superiors and his political officers, even when their orders entail the sacrifice of his private interests to the needs of the Party and the progress of the revolution. Comrade Lotnik, your recent behaviour indicates that you have failed on all counts.'

There then followed a lecture on the infallibility of the Party, the supremacy of its needs and the unquestioning obedience it demanded of its members and supporters. I knew the text as well as he did. When at last he had finished, he moved back to his desk, sat down and began to study my records for a second time. I continued to stand to attention, staring straight ahead at the wall opposite. Eventually he spoke again.

'Given your record, I am especially disappointed in your behaviour, comrade Lotnik. I see that you volunteered to join the Air Force and that you used to be a partisan under General Kolpakov.'

(This was not strictly true: General Kolpakov had led the Soviet partisans on Polish territory and I had exaggerated the Peasants' Battalions' collaboration with them, making out that we had fought primarily with them. Fortunately, nobody was in a position to check on my story.)

'I see you were wounded, captured by the Nazis and survived a concentration camp. Your record up to now has been good. It would be a pity to throw it all away.'

His change of tack gave me renewed hope. Perhaps, after all, he was not going to punish me.

'Do you still want to be of service to the Party and to a free, democratic Poland?'

'More than anything else in the world, comrade lieutenant,' I replied. 'I volunteered so that I could serve my country, comrade lieutenant, and help to liberate it from the Nazis, who have persecuted me and my family.'

He remained impassive. Then, without changing his expression or softening his tone, he came to the point. 'As you seem to be a capable young man, I am inclined to overlook your lapse of discipline.'

I breathed out heavily and the first traces of a smile began to spread over my lips as I began to think how I should thank him before he indicated with his eyes that I should keep my mouth shut.

'You may have a great future ahead of you, comrade Lotnik, if I give you the opportunity now to make up for your misconduct, but you must repay this generosity by dedicating your life to the Party. You know that if you are ready to help the Party, the Party will do all it can to help you.'

He paused and I judged it wise to wait for a signal before I responded in any way.

'You know that the Party has many enemies who scheme to subvert its work, to undermine the success of the revolution and to re-install the capitalist order. The Party must be watchful at all times and on all fronts in order to catch these enemies, who are at work within the Air Force too, among both Poles and Russians. If you want to serve the Party, then the best thing you can do is to help us investigate our enemies and bring them to justice. If you wish to help the Party in this way, then the Party will see that you get out of your present difficulties. What would you say if I proposed sending you to Chkalov for a few weeks?'

'It would be an honour to go there,' I stammered, utterly unprepared for this sudden turn in his questioning. Chkalov, deep inside the Soviet Union, was the most prestigious training centre for pilots in the whole of the Soviet Union and had a reputation like that of Sandhurst or West Point: it was for the elite. My mind raced to understand the implications of his proposal.

Then he spelt them out.

'If you go to Chkalov, you will learn to be vigilant on behalf of the Party in order to protect the revolution from traitors and saboteurs. You will learn how to use your eyes and ears for the Party until they do the Party's work for it instinctively. You will learn how to understand the hidden thoughts of others and to find out their true beliefs and intentions. You will learn how to obtain information on the Party's enemies by scrutinising the behaviour of your supposed comrades and by listening to their conversations. Even though the Party's enemies are everywhere, it takes skill and bravery to identify them swiftly and reliably. You will also learn utter and absolute discretion, which means you will never breathe a word about this conversation or about anything you see in Chkalov to another living creature except me. You will report anything and everything that you learn to me and only to me. From now on your official status will be that of an NKVD undercover agent.'

My mind buzzed with such excitement that I stood no chance of assimilating the significance of what he had just said. Later I remembered the way he had smiled when I had refused to go to church. That must have been when he had first noticed me.

When he had finished, there was only one thing I could think of asking. 'What about my training to be a pilot?' I said. 'I want to serve democratic Poland by helping to defeat the Nazis as a pilot.'

'If you want to become a pilot so that you can serve the Party, then I will see to it that the Party helps you become a pilot.'

I looked puzzled and he explained.

'We can always arrange extra flying hours for you when you return.'

He continued with the more practical arrangements.

'I will have to make a show of punishing you so as not to arouse suspicion. I will announce that you have four weeks' detention for absence without leave. That will cover your time in Chkalov.'

After he had finished he ordered an officer to march me to the detention centre, where I was to be locked up for twenty-four hours. The next day I would be transferred to the bakery, ostensibly for four weeks' hard labour, from where I would be fetched in the evening. That way I would be seen in two different locations, in case anybody wondered where I had been and felt tempted to compare notes with others. Confusion was thus sown; everything planned with cunning and efficiency. I had no objections, as I still felt I had escaped a much worse fate, if not death, by a whisker.

In the detention centre I was shoved into a cell measuring approximately six feet by nine with no furniture and no window. It was a concrete box in which the prisoner was expected to stand or sit for twenty-four hours a day, except for visits to the latrines at the end of the corridor. Food seemed to be served at irregular intervals. At about nine o'clock a warder passed me a wooden pallet, on which I was supposed to sleep until six o'clock the next morning. There was no mattress or pillow and I had only my thick, regulation-issue coat for a blanket, but at least I did not have to lie down on the icy-cold concrete floor.

On the way to the latrines shortly after arrival I passed another prisoner and took advantage of the warder's momentary distraction to snatch a brief conversation with him. He dragged his left foot, which was wrapped in dirty cloth, behind him, his swollen face showed several weeks' growth of beard, though it was not cut or bruised, and his ragged clothes hung loosely from his emaciated body. It was clearly a matter of a week or two until he died of hunger, cold and exhaustion. As he edged past me on his way back to his cell, I realised that I recognised him. We had enlisted together in Lublin back in August and had got to know each other quite well by dint of our enforced proximity. He had then become one of those who had disappeared mysteriously in the night and I had forgotten all about him. No one had ever mentioned his name again and, like everybody else, I had quickly forgotten all about him. I was taken aback to find him in the dungeons because I knew his enthusiasm to fight the Nazis was at least as great as mine.

'What have they done to you?' I asked him.

'They haven't done anything to me. They just asked me a few questions and locked me up in here.'

'Have you asked to see a doctor?'

'Of course I have.'

He mumbled his words in a hoarse whisper and let me know that six weeks in a cold, damp cell with inadequate food, no light, no chair, no bed and no means of keeping warm had been quite enough to transform a fit, healthy man into this worn-out shell. He had just been left there to rot. The mere fact that it was impossible to sit or lie down during the day, except on the cold, hard concrete, had been enough to paralyse his left arm and leg. Although he felt that his gaolers had thrown away the key to his cell and he had not been charged with an offence, he knew they had not forgotten him entirely, as he frequently found that he failed to get a bowl of gruel when the other prisoners were fed.

'They've got it in for me. They single me out for special treatment. Me and a couple of others.'

I felt sorry for him because he had been a likeable, talkative fellow, but someone had obviously denounced him for something or other he had allegedly said or done.

After a day's work in the bakery I was taken back to my cell from where an officer fetched me the following day to take me to a small passenger aircraft that stood waiting on the runway. The plane held eight people in addition to the pilot and co-pilot. For a Polish officer cadet, especially one who had spent the previous night in a freezing cell and who twenty-four hours earlier had half-expected to be deported to Siberia, I now found myself in unusual company. The half-dozen other passengers were all high-ranking Russian officers who joked with each other occasionally during the five-hour flight, although none of them addressed as much as a word to me.

On arrival in Chkalov I was led immediately to my quarters, a two-bedded, centrally-heated room, which I was to share with a Russian lieutenant who had also just arrived. I could not remember the last time I had slept in such luxury: the contrast with the cell I had occupied the previous night or with the drafty barracks in Zamosc could not have been greater. Another even greater luxury lay in store, however. After an hour's physical exercise in the morning, wearing nothing but boots, trousers and vest to fend off the dread temperatures of the Russian winter, we washed in hot water. In Zamosc someone had to break the ice on the water barrels before anybody could wash at all. It goes without saying that the food was also first-rate.

Three or four students in my class of 30 were Poles, while the rest were Soviet citizens from as far away as Siberia and Kazakhstan. Some of these Soviets spoke Russian very poorly, which meant that lectures could be laboriously slow. Some had been to Chkalov before and had returned for refresher courses, but the majority consisted of novices like myself, most of them due back at the front once the course had finished. We were all strangers to each other and remained strangers, using first names only, since any sort of friendship was frowned upon. Each agent would operate independently in the future and none of us would know who else in his unit, regiment or squadron worked for the NKVD. Only the superior officer knew how many operatives he had under him, and even he could be sure that others in turn kept him under surveillance and reported on him to headquarters at regular intervals. The NKVD had thousand upon thousand of informers, possibly as many as one in four in Zamosc, though I never succeeded in identifying another one. The men and women in Chkalov belonged to a different category, however.

This was the upper stratum of the network: we were agents, not simply stooges.

Despite the favourable physical conditions, my main memory of Chkalov is of tiredness and overwork, as we were kept to a punishing schedule. After five hours' sleep and an hour's exercise, lecture followed lecture all day with barely a break. When an instructor noticed that heads were beginning to nod, which happened frequently during the long day, the best he could suggest was a ten-minute jog outside. This was effective in so far as the sudden change in temperature, as much as 40 degrees centigrade, jolted would-be sleepers back to wakefulness. The cold air stabbed the throat and lungs, yet after an hour back inside a well-heated room the tiredness returned worse than ever.

After breakfast came political theory: more Stalin, Lenin and Marx, all of them familiar to me from Zamosc. In Chkalov, however, I realised how important the order of priority was for the Russians. First came the Party, which always came above all its functionaries, no matter how high they had risen, then the Revolution, and then Stalin and Lenin, followed by Marx and Engels. That was the strict order of things. In the 1930s Stalin had been the Party's General Secretary; now he had been elevated to Father and Saviour of the Nation and had assumed semi-divine status – the cult of the personality, his critics called it.

The lecturers made the doctrine as simple as possible for us, dictated notes for hours on end and wrote key words and phrases on the blackboard, insisting, however, that we read the necessary books for ourselves. The well-stocked library contained all the Russian classical authors in addition to the socialist thinkers and they expected us to spend any spare time with a book in front of us. Everything had to be learnt by heart, revised and recited over and over again and then regurgitated once the appropriate prompt was given. Their first objective was to get us to think instinctively along Party lines and to make it our second nature to serve the Party, the state and the new society we were in the process of building. Any independence of thought, any critical spirit, any bourgeois or individualist notion had to be eradicated.

They also sought to raise our self-esteem by praising us endlessly for having been chosen from thousands of others to serve the Party in this essential way. Without us the revolution would fail, as our contribution saved the Party from destruction at the hands of its enemies. We were the indispensable guardians of the most democratic system in the world and our work was the purest, cleanest type of work because we received no special reward for it. Our efforts went unsung and could never be recognised in public, since this would immediately invalidate our achievements. In fact, the mere mention of reward would be tantamount to a suggestion of bribery and the socialist system could never be corrupt: it rewarded merit and merit alone.

In the afternoons and evenings the subject changed to methods of detection and intelligence-gathering, which I found much more stimulating than political theory. In this field the NKVD instructors certainly knew what they were talking about: their subtleties stood in contrast to the brute force favoured by the Gestapo. The first basic rule was that nobody, not even a brother, a sister or the closest childhood friend, could be trusted. Any individual, even a close relative, who spoke or acted in any way suspiciously had to be reported to a superior without delay.

The second basic rule was that no agent had the power to act independently, and even superior officers had no right to proceed on their own. Instead they had to let the Party, which had the courts at its disposal, decide on the guilt or innocence of the accused. On the other hand, agents had to learn how to cultivate new friendships and win the confidence of others. Within earshot of others they were forbidden to use anti-Communist language or criticise the Party, as this might undermine morale, but once an agent was alone with his quarry he might tempt him to reveal his true feelings or beliefs by pretending to hold anti-Communist views himself. If a suspect was gregarious, the agent's objective was always to prise him away from his friends, to get him drinking on his own by suggesting an outing to a secluded night-spot where no one could overhear the conversation.

As political discussions were encouraged at all times, it was sometimes easy to catch out an unsuspecting individual. If, for example, someone said that the intelligentsia had played its part in the Revolution and continued to make a valuable contribution to society, the agent should agree and encourage the man to carry on. A chance remark like that, in praise of a social group which was now the declared enemy of the people and the Revolution, could have fatal consequences for the man who uttered it. If he realised his blunder and tried to cover it up by making remarks critical of the intelligentsia, this could lead him into even greater danger, as it showed that he knew Party doctrine and was aware how dangerous his previous views sounded. If, on the other hand, he proved hopelessly ignorant and contradicted himself at every turn, then the agent might justifiably conclude that stupidity alone had led him to make his original comment.

When drinking with a suspect, the agent had to know how much alcohol he himself could take, plan perhaps to tip part of his drink away and then fake drunkenness, babbling made-up sympathy for the Nazis in order to test his companion's reaction. All our energies were to be concentrated on making people trip themselves up and say things that they had not meant to say. The virtues of patience and perseverance distinguished an NKVD officer; discretion and secrecy were also highly-prized qualities.

Towards the end of the four weeks we took part in classroom demonstrations of investigative techniques. Students came to the front of the class and acted out discussions with a suspect, while the rest made notes and prepared to comment upon the performance. Another basic rule was never ever to ask a direct question, never to say or do anything which might arouse suspicion, as the person under investigation could well have enjoyed training at the hands of Western intelligence services and would himself be on the look-out. Nor must the agent ever show too much interest in the discussion but instead feign a casual lack of concern and make out that he would prefer to discuss a different subject altogether.

First of all: find out the suspect's weaknesses or preferences. If you already know the person, you must begin by telling him about something you know he likes – in the Air Force this usually meant flying missions, women or drink – before steering the conversation in the direction you wanted it to go. If a man liked going out with women, then you could mention a place you knew where there were girls galore and wait for him to ask where it was. Never press an invitation upon him. Instead wait for him to pester you with questions and then give the information reluctantly, saying that you don't have time to take him over the next few days. 'Keep him dangling' was the motto. Never, never let on that you want him to come with you. There were several women in the class, all of them pretty, and no secret was made of the fact that they were expected to exploit their physical attractiveness in defence of the Revolution.

The NKVD wanted to get the remaining 'fascists' in our midst if they posed a threat to the new democratic state, as they feared fascist sabotage allied to Western infiltration. Revenge played a minor part in their plans and I think that they even considered retribution for war crimes to be something of a bourgeois luxury, as the war was still far from over and they knew that it would take them time to establish their rule in their newly conquered territories. Capitalists and the bourgeoisie also featured on the NKVD target lists, but the political lecturers never referred to individual Western countries by name. They said only 'the West' or 'the capitalist West' when telling us about cigar-smoking factory owners surrounded by servants and mountains of food and caring nothing for their starving, maltreated workers, who themselves dreamed of Soviet pay and employment conditions.

The prospect of having to report Nazi collaborators did not alarm me in the slightest. On the contrary, I considered it my duty to see that Nazi sympathisers, whether now active or inactive, received their come-uppance. Some of the stories about the West made sense to me when I thought of pre-war Poland, and some of the other propaganda rubbed off as well. I believed, just as my instructors and lecturers did, that all people were born equal and deserved the same chances in life. To my mind, the fact that the Soviet Union sought to integrate its great variety of peoples, including now the Polish people, into its system made it far preferable to the Third Reich, which viewed all Slavs as an inferior species.

My experiences in Chkalov also served to boost my confidence in my own abilities and I began to realise that as long as I knew the rules of the game, I could manipulate them for my own advantage, however dangerous the game itself might be. As the political commissars always had to watch what they themselves said, it was sometimes easy to turn Party doctrine back on them. Conversely, as I remembered the refugees from the pre-war Bolshevik Ukraine who had streamed across the Polish border with tales of horror and famine, I was also aware that they did not practise all that they preached. I knew that my family faced difficulties and that a cousin of mine in Zakzrouvek had been deported. As a result my feelings towards our new Soviet rulers continued to be ambivalent.

The end of the course coincided with a great military parade and the longest cavalcade of limousines I had ever seen. Word passed round that the *Gaspadin* (The Boss) was likely to make an appearance, but nobody could tell which car might contain him. *Gaspadin* was one of many different names people called him in public, all of which added to his awesome mystique and superhuman reputation: he was The Father, The Infallible, The Conqueror of the Fascist Scourge, The Victor over the Hitlerites, The Great Comrade and The Saviour of the Nation, even before the war had finished. The top brass from Chkalov lined up at the front of the airstrip, the rest of us three or four abreast in columns behind them.

As the two dozen identical limousines swept through the gates, the whisper passed down the lines that the man with the many names, Tovarisch Stalin, was riding in one of them. When the cars drew to a halt, the doors to all but one of them swung open and uniformed officers leapt out to open the doors of the remaining vehicle. Stalin marched briskly in front of his phalanx of bodyguards, several generals following a few paces behind. By now everyone on the parade ground realised who he was. An NKVD general cried 'Hip! Hip!' and 4,000 voices shouted 'Hurrah!' in a deep, booming roar. Four thousand winter hats were hurled into the air. The hat-throwing and shouting continued for almost a minute until Stalin gestured with both hands for quiet. An aide held a microphone to his mouth and he began to speak. I have never forgotten his words.

'Comrades, I have always believed that our Soviet falcon would vanquish the German vulture. Thanks to your skill and dedication to the Party, our glorious Red Army will soon be at the gates of Berlin. I have always had faith in our Air Force and in our pilots and I have always known that they would defend our democratic Motherland with their lives and would defeat the Hitlerite bandits and Nazi murderers. Victory is soon to be ours.'

Somebody shouted, 'Long live Our Saviour and Guide! Long live the Infallible Comrade Stalin! Long live the Soviet Motherland!'

Four thousand hats flew into the air once again and the 'Hurrahs!' echoed even more deafeningly than before. 'The Infallible' himself applauded, as was the Soviet custom, by stretching out his hands towards the crowd. After the noise had begun to subside, he waved, turned smartly on his heel and walked back to his car. I cheered as loudly as anyone.

Two days later I was back in Zamosc. We flew back in a Douglas, an aircraft donated by the American allies. This time the plane contained a colonel and a couple of lower-ranking officers returning to the front from military hospitals. Ordinary soldiers, had they been sent home for medical treatment, which in itself was unlikely, would have been obliged to hitch lifts on military vehicles, which made me feel extremely pampered and important. Before I left, the NKVD gave me some new Polish currency (the first time I had ever been paid) and I looked forward to the prospect of further instalments.

It was still early evening and I wanted to slip back into the camp after lights out, so I had time on my hands and went into Zamosc with the intention of finding a woman. The combination of an officer's uniform and money made this easy and I took my pick. After we had spent a few minutes in the back-room of a seedy establishment, she begged me to come back to her home and to bring my friends the next time. I need not have paid her any money – a drink or two was all she wanted. Drinks were as good as free for uniformed cadets and women were ready to go with a soldier in return for a free evening at his side. I told her I was in a hurry and crept back into the base at about eleven o'clock, taking a side entrance into the commissar's building.

I found Schlomin working at his desk. He put away his gun when he recognised me.

'How did you get on?' he asked.

'I liked it, comrade lieutenant.'

'Did anybody see you come in just now?'

'No.'

'You can go.'

'But what are my instructions?'

'Not tonight. We'll deal with that at the right time. Remember, you have been on work detail. If anyone asks, say you've just been released.'

'Where shall I sleep?'

'Just find an empty bed in your barracks. Yours has been taken. In the morning just carry on as normal. I will get in touch with you when the time is right.'

'Yes, comrade lieutenant'.

'Good night, comrade Lotnik.'

'Good night, comrade lieutenant.'

I had expected to be issued with orders straightaway and set to work on somebody, but the NKVD never did anything in a rush. Schlomin had taken my inexperience into account and did not want anyone, not even one of his own officers, to suspect that I was an agent. He was the only person who knew where I had been.

It was two whole weeks before he was in touch and instructed me to carry out routine observations on the men in my squadron, in particular to find out what contacts they kept in the town, whether they had steady girlfriends and whether they went with the crowd or preferred to keep themselves to themselves. Schlomin went over a few of the tactics I had learnt in Chkalov.

'If a man doesn't join in the sexual banter or the boasting about how much vodka he can hold, that in itself isn't an indication that he has subversive tendencies. Yet he might have reasons for his reserve and you must watch him and find out if he has, and, if so, what they are.'

On the other hand, a loudmouth who suddenly went quiet and no longer took part in the drinking sessions he had previously orchestrated might also have something on his conscience. I kept my eyes and ears open and continued to play my full part in extra-curricular activities which, in our rare free evenings, consisted solely of drinking and womanising.

By Christmas I still had nothing to report, which began to worry me. This was either because I was a novice and needed more practice or because nobody in my squadron had any secrets worth discovering. My unwillingness to inform on someone for anything less than collaboration with the German or Ukrainian Nazis must have contributed to my failure, as my own commitment to the cause of what the Soviets told us would be a free and democratic Poland was founded on the Red Army defeating Germany. Still, I realised that Schlomin would want results sooner or later. Fortunately, I was soon presented with an opportunity to take a close interest in a couple of my comrades.

In the New Year I went down with pneumonia after foolishly agreeing to box a challenger for a couple of rounds and afterwards, in the glow of victory, standing, my body still dripping with sweat, in the freezing cold for more than half an hour. I had to spend more than a week in the base hospital at Deblin, where we had moved shortly beforehand. For three days the fever made me delirious, but I subsequently made a quick recovery and regained my strength.

In the corner of the single ward two Poles held whispered conversations long into the night. I caught snippets of their exchanges and became suspicious when I realised they spoke of everyday subjects in voices loud enough for me and others to hear, only to sink to a whisper every now and then. I made out enough to understand that they were boasting to one another about how well off they had been during the German occupation. One said his family had a luxury car at its disposal because his father had been a top government official. They reminisced about the food they had bought and mutual friends from pre-war times, yet they never discussed Russia, the Eastern Front or anything else to do with the military.

I became convinced they had collaborated with the Nazis and, through a process of elimination, worked out that they had probably served in the Wehrmacht or the SS as *Volksdeutsche*. Nothing else seemed to fit. After release from hospital, I checked the place, date and the unit which they had originally joined from their recruitment documents, which were readily available to me. I discovered they had enlisted into Berling's Polish army in the spring of 1944 at a spot near the pre-war Russo-Polish border, some 700 miles from Silesia. I knew for a fact that Berling's army contained very few Silesians at that point, as it consisted either of Poles liberated from the Nazi camps, POWs captured by the Soviets in 1939 or ethnic Poles from the Soviet Union. My original suspicions were strengthened. All they would have had to do when their German unit surrendered was discard their uniforms and pose as Polish victims of Nazism. There were thousands who switched sides in that way.

After my illness I had even more flying time to catch up on and found myself way behind most of the others in the technical subjects. The lecturer never even bothered to ask me any questions, knowing that I would not give the correct answer. I was determined to succeed, however, and decided to learn all the equations and formulae by heart, which resulted in my astounding him one day by knowing the answer to a question. From then on he took a greater interest in me and made sure that I grasped the main points of the lectures. These efforts left me with little time to follow my two suspects and Schlomin was not particularly pleased when he called me to his office a week later.

'You've not exactly exerted yourself, have you?' he said to me with unaccustomed sarcasm.

I told him I had been in hospital for a week and so had to catch up with my work and training. He knew all about my illness and had also heard that I had started to make better progress in class, but he remained unimpressed.

'I hope I haven't wasted my efforts on you. We need results, not excuses. In a week you'll be moving to a different aerodrome and by then I want you to have something to tell me.'

I then told him that I had two very promising leads which I hoped would produce information shortly.

'Let's hope they're worth something,' he replied as I left his office.

Ten days later he glanced at me in the yard, which was the signal that I should follow him. This time he was even less good-tempered than at our last meeting and told me I had been slack in my work. Although I had nothing more on the two suspects than what I had picked up in the hospital, I passed on the name of one of them, Babitsch, and explained what I had found out about him. He noted the name and said that he hoped that his trust in me was at last beginning to pay off.

'Let's hope that in future you'll be more productive. You won't be able to follow the suspect any further because we are sending the squadron to Uleze in a week's time.'

His way of instilling a sense of responsibility in me was to give me advance knowledge of our movements, which no one else in the squadron knew.

'I have special tasks for you there. The region east of Warsaw is infested with anti-Communist forces, who still control the forests and the countryside. In addition to watching individuals in the squadron, I want you to fraternise with the local population and tell me where their sympathies lie.'

Whenever I now returned to Deblin from Uleze, I took steps

to avoid Schlomin. In turn he rarely troubled me. Unfortunately, there was a second man called Babitsch in the squadron, a lieutenant who had conducted some of our flying classes. He had been in the Red Air Force since 1941. When I saw him marching with the ranks on the parade ground rather than barking the orders, my heart stopped. The most likely scenario sped through my head. I started up a conversation with a Kazak who was in Babitsch's company, trying to make my voice sound as casual as possible, and asked him what had happened to Babitsch, pretending I had not seen him since my transfer to Uleze.

'Oh, he's still flying with us, but he's not as hot as we thought he would be and he doesn't give any lessons any more,' came the reply.

'What do you mean? He's been trained already. He's been in combat.'

'Between you and me,' the man replied in hushed tones, 'I don't think he'll make a good pilot. The only reason he was here in the first place was because he's a Party member.'

That made the mistake, if mistake it had been, all the more serious. Someone who was not a Party member would have been taken out and deported simply on the basis of a tip-off. Schlomin had put the wrong Babitsch under investigation, demoting him for as long as it took to find out that he was clean. Then he would come back to me for passing on unreliable information. The Party never made mistakes. I could not go to Schlomin because this would reveal that I had noticed what he had done, which could not be questioned. I reckoned I had a few weeks before the investigations ended. Once I had got my wings I could put in for a transfer and get out of his way.

From time to time Schlomin would give me the name of someone he wanted me to follow. If one of his informers had passed on a lead to him, my task was to see where the information led. I normally took about a week before reporting back to him that the man in question was politically as hard as steel and a dedicated Communist but that he sometimes drank too much and got out of control or that his sexual appetite got the better of him to the point that he was inclined to use physical force to make a woman submit. This sort of information usually satisfied Schlomin and got him off my back. I refused to be responsible for a man's downfall or death, unless I knew he had been a Nazi, in which case I felt no compunction.

Meanwhile the couple of months spent in Uleze turned out to be a holiday. The Russians decamped every night to their quarters in Deblin as they reckoned that the aerodrome was too dangerous for them, and at weekends the Polish cadets were free to mix with the locals. The first and most arduous stage of the training was now over and we were flying Yaks and Stormoviks for an hour or two each day. Unlike Zamosc and most of the county of Lublin, Uleze and the surrounding villages had not suffered heavily from partisan activity and Nazi reprisals. The people here had seen nothing like the Polish-Ukrainian slaughter and basic foodstuffs had been in reasonable supply throughout most of the war. The peasants had managed to hide most of their livestock from the Germans, who had been content to guard their aerodrome and keep out of the surrounding forest. When we entered a local café, salami and vodka were immediately placed on the table and it was almost unthinkable for a charge to be made. The people were simply relieved that the war was over. The young women were ready to be shown a good time by the airmen, all the more so as their boyfriends were either dead or still working in German factories. We cadets took full advantage of the imbalance between the sexes. Our uniforms gave us a glamour which made seduction easy, but after so much killing, many people just lived for the day. I remember asking one woman who had invited me to spend the night with her to bring me something to ease my throbbing hangover the following morning. She came back with a mug of squash laced with vodka and wanted to start celebrating all over again.

My accomplice in these exploits was a man from Vilnius named Orlowski. Sometimes we drank all through the night and talked so much that we did not bother to go in search of girls. On another occasion we ended up sharing the bed of a generous twenty-year-old, who told us we would have to work in shifts in order to satisfy her. One night when we had decided to stay inside the barracks, he turned to me as he opened the second bottle of the evening.

'You're very close to Schlomin, aren't you?'

'What do you mean?' I said. 'Do you think he's supplying me with illegal drink?'

We laughed and he did not follow up his question. Since I drank more than he did that night, he doubtless thought that I was too drunk to notice what he was saying. I did notice, but unfortunately I was too stupid to think anything more of it.

At the end of the first week of May 1945 I was summoned to Deblin and told to await new instructions. I waited two days and two nights for the orders to come through. On the third evening, a couple of hours after sunset and after the Polish companies, now separated from their Russian comrades, had retired to bed, we all leapt from our bunks on hearing a series of explosions going off no more than a quarter of a mile away. My first thought was that the Home Army had attacked the base. The sky was alight with flares, which usually signalled an attack, but they were letting off everything at once – tanks, artillery and rifles. It made no military sense at all.

Schlomin had turned quite pale, but proved that he did not lack courage. He knew that at least a third of the Poles on the base hated him and would not hesitate to join the attackers, yet he ordered us to take up positions at strategic points on the perimeter fence. He told me to command a group defending the main gate while he led the other two groups to the opposite side.

'You want me to command my class, comrade lieutenant?' I asked him incredulously, as there were at least a dozen men superior to me whom he could have asked.

'That's an order!' he shouted.

'And do you expect us to stave them off with rifles? The machine guns are back in the aerodrome.'

'Get to the main gate and do what you can!' he yelled back.

His hands continued to shake, while I felt quite relaxed – if the nationalists were attacking, then they would not shoot Poles.

By the time I had taken my men to the main gate, the shooting had already abated somewhat and the threat of an all-out attack seemed to have receded, at least temporarily. Nevertheless, we expected the worst. Then Schlomin emerged from the direction of the HQ, smiling broadly, his hands no longer shaking and with the colour returned to his face.

'There's no emergency. We must celebrate. Germany has surrendered – the war's over!'

We had mistaken the universal jubilation for a military attack.

The end of the war in Europe made little difference to the daily routine, however. While danger still lurked round every corner, I returned to Uleze and resumed both flying practice and my former dissolute life. A week or so later a large gang of us descended on a dance in the firemen's hall of a local village. Usually we split up into smaller groups so as not to overwhelm the local population, but this dance was big enough for that not to be necessary. Shortly after the dancing started, the festivities were brought to a swift halt by the sudden entrance of a clutch of NKVD officers. A captain marched to the front of the hall as the dancers fell silent.

'What's going on?' a Polish cadet yelled at them. 'We're celebrating the end of the war and you enter the building as if you think you own it.'

'We will let the festivities continue as soon as our business is complete,' the captain replied.

'Law-abiding citizens need have nothing to fear,' he went on. 'At the request of the Polish internal security organisations and the Polish authorities we are looking for deserters. Any man born between 1924 and 1925 who has received his call-up papers and not registered for the military is now a deserter.'

He gave a speech on the virtues of the Soviet Union before his men began to inspect the documents of every man present.

'Women and military personnel may remain where they are.

Any men who haven't got identity papers with them may send someone home to fetch them.'

The entire village was surrounded and escape was as good as impossible. Still, the NKVD strategy contained a high element of risk, as the Poles heavily outnumbered them. We moved outside. As they filled four lorries with reluctant conscripts, I dared not go too close for fear I would not be able to control my anger. A man of about my age saw his chance and made a run for the woods half a mile in the distance. He zigzagged expertly to avoid the rifle fire and, once he had got 500 yards, turned round and called back, 'Here's a better target for you.' He then pulled down his trousers and displayed his backside, to the immense amusement of the Polish cadets and the evident embarrassment of the Russians.

A young woman brought a jacket outside for her arrested brother, but the NKVD officer at first refused her permission to hand it to him. One of our officers went over to translate for them and in the end, after she had showed that nothing was hidden in the jacket, she was allowed to pass it to her brother. A Russian driver made a vulgar remark to her, which made me want to wring his neck. If we only had a couple of dozen partisans, I thought to myself, a machine gun or two and some hand-grenades, we could soon sort out this lot.

They drove off, taking several dozen men with them, and the rest of us quickly dispersed. Shaken by what had happened, Orlowski and I wandered to the next village and found a bar. Before we had become even slightly tipsy, he turned to speak.

'Look, I want to confide in you. What I have to say could cost me my life.'

'Well,' I answered, 'think twice before you say anything.'

'We've been friends for such a long time, I want to tell you. You remember the man without a jacket? He approached me as the NKVD arrived and handed me a bundle, saying it contained documents and a pistol. "If they find it on me, I'm a dead man and hundreds of others will have their lives put at risk." He gave me the name of someone waiting outside who I should give the bundle to. I did exactly as he said.'

I assured him his information was safe with me and thought to myself that, had I been in his shoes, I would have done the same. We carried on drinking and polished off a litre of vodka each before he went off to a field with a woman. He told me to wait for him and I remember the sight of his backside flashing up and down in the moonlight. It surprised me that he was still up to it after all the drink he had consumed.

We slept it off the next morning and I put what he had told me to the back of my mind. He was my closest friend and I realised that what he had done could easily have him convicted for treason. I even felt flattered that he had confided in me.

A week later Schlomin sent a dispatch rider from Deblin summoning me to see him. I was told there was urgent business we had to discuss and I packed a few belongings and waited at the main gate for a lorry, as the rider had sped off after delivering his message. I arrived at Deblin at lunchtime and found Schlomin on his way to the mess. As he had ordered me to see him, I did not care who saw us talking to one another. He told me to accompany him to the mess.

'I haven't heard anything from you for over a month. What's the matter? Aren't you satisfied? I made sure you passed your exams. You've got your wings now and you've been avoiding me ever since.'

'That's not true,' I protested. 'I don't want to waste your time when I have nothing to report.'

'How's it going in Uleze?'

'Fine. I'm looking forward to flying again,' I said.

'That might be some time off now that the war is over.'

Then he asked me who my friends were and whom I was concentrating on at that moment. I replied that I was working on nobody in particular.

'There are only about 30 of us and I know all of them. They seem perfectly reliable to me. One or two are not so keen on making friends and keep themselves to themselves, and I have yet to investigate them as thoroughly as I would like. There are bits and pieces of trivia I have overheard, but nothing which is going to damage the Party or Soviet-Polish relations.'

I was hoping he would not notice my nervousness and was dying for him to come to the point. We walked slowly. Once he thought he had given me enough time, he asked me whether I knew Orlowski.

'What do you think of him?'

'Oh, he seems a reliable sort. He's a good pilot and comes from a solid peasant family,' I stammered. I should have said that we were best friends.

'So, you're not on intimate terms with him?'

At this point I began to get suspicious. I denied the truth and said that we were merely acquaintances. He had to drag the rest of the information out of me, as he wanted to know exactly how well the two of us knew each other and what we had done together. He was a master of the casual approach.

When we finally reached the mess room, he told me to go and eat in the aviation officers' mess.

'Have your lunch and meet me just after two o'clock.'

I turned round and went to obey his instructions, my head well and truly muddled by all that I had heard. I noticed that I was being watched by the base informer, the man known to one and all to report everything he heard directly to his superiors. He beckoned in my direction.

'Psst!'

I assumed he meant someone else, as I had barely ever addressed a word to him. The last thing I wanted was to talk to him. He beckoned again and there was no mistaking that he wanted to speak to me. I walked towards him and he quickened his step so as to keep a few paces ahead of me.

'Walk normally,' he told me without looking around. 'Don't let anyone see we are talking. I have only one thing to say to you. Your number's up. Your friend has betrayed you. Orlowski is a traitor.'

'What do you mean? What can I do?' My mind was taking its time to absorb what he had said.

'Just get the hell out of here.'

I walked first towards the mess room in case anyone else was watching, then turned and went in the direction of the main gate without arousing suspicion by walking any faster. Once out of the gate, I got to the station and jumped onto a train going to Zamosc.

Of all the surprises in my life, this one took me the longest to understand. A man I believed to be a spineless stooge had saved my life; the man I regarded as my best friend had tried to have me arrested. The story about the man with the bundle had been a test. In my foolishness, I had failed that test, but been rescued by a most unlikely saviour.

9

The Free Cavalry,
May–July 1945

Stalin ordered the exchange of people living on either side of
the Bug soon after the Red Army crossed the river in July 1944.
Ukrainians from Poland made their way east to settle in
Volhynia, Galicia and even further afield, piling their possessions onto horse-drawn carts and leaving the villages their
families had inhabited for centuries. Poles who had survived
the wave of atrocities east of the Bug moved in the opposite
direction, either occupying abandoned Ukrainian villages in
Poland or going in search of homes in the new Polish territories in the west – Silesia, Pomerania and the renamed city of
Gdansk, all of which Poland gained from Germany after the
previous inhabitants had in their turn been moved further
west.

Polish and Ukrainian carts passed each other on the roads,
identical in most respects, except for the quantity of goods
which the owners had managed to salvage from their farmsteads or pillage from abandoned houses and settlements. In
the main, the Ukrainians had emerged victorious despite the
defeat of Nazism. East of the Bug, where Polish civilians had not
enjoyed partisan protection to the same extent as on the west
bank of the river, and where they had suffered far graver
assaults over a longer period than in the county of Lublin, the
ceding of territory from Poland to the Soviet Union confirmed

the supremacy of the Ukrainians, hitherto supported by the Nazis. The war between the two sides would come to an end only when they were separated once and for all by a border.

As the Soviets shot all non-Germans they captured in Nazi uniform, Ukrainian militia members, camp guards and members of the SS divisions all fled west to places where no one knew them, where they could be issued with new papers and even claim to have been victims of the Nazis. Many fled Poland altogether to settle in the West. Meanwhile reprisals and counter-reprisals continued sporadically. One, which claimed the lives of some of my former comrades from the Peasants' Battalion, had taken place on Palm Sunday 1945, some six weeks before my desertion from the Red Air Force. The plaque in the village on the western side of the Bug commemorating the victims records that 41 people perished in the raid.

The survivors from my unit, about 50 of the men I knew, including the CO, had continued to fight until the liberation, when the Soviets encharged a section of them with a citizens' militia station. Their task was to keep order and to protect local Poles from roving Ukrainians, precisely what they had been doing for the previous two years.

On Palm Sunday the Catholic village church was full for the first free celebration of Holy Week in six years. Perhaps the priest drew parallels in his sermon between Christ's entry into Jerusalem and Poland's deliverance from Nazism, as the devout and non-devout alike gave thanks that the war was nearing its end. But as the congregation filed out of the church, two trucks pulled up to unload a platoon of men dressed in NKVD uniforms. They went straight to the militia station, ordered the men outside and bundled them into the vehicles. Before leaving, they tossed grenades into the horrified crowd of worshippers emerging from church and sprayed them with bullets. The platoon did not come from the NKVD at all: this was a Ukrainian band still crazy for blood. Had my ex-comrades realised their identity, they would never have let themselves be taken alive, as a slow death by torture awaited them. Their bodies were never recovered. Thus it was that my trusted CO survived the main fighting only to perish with his men in liberated Polish territory five weeks before the final defeat of Nazi Germany.

On my last leave before my narrow escape from Schlomin's wrath, I arrived in Hrubieszow for three days just after Easter and heard news of this latest atrocity, but there was little time to grieve. After spending a night at Aunt Sophie's house, I bumped into an old friend, Bartek, a distant cousin on my mother's side. He was a couple of years older than me and, having escaped the forced-labour round-ups, had spent most of the war as a messenger for the Home Army. He still ran errands and passed messages for them, as the underground network was yet to be disarmed, let alone disbanded. While Home Army groups had by and large not yet taken up arms against the new occupiers, they acted as self-appointed policemen, safeguarding the welfare of the Poles against both the old Ukrainian enemy and, increasingly, the prying attention of the Soviet secret police. Meanwhile they waited, like all true Polish patriots, for the Western powers to keep their promise and establish an independent Polish state. When the moment was ripe, Polish patriots would know what to do and would be ready to do whatever was necessary.

After warm embraces and enquiries about mutual friends and relatives, Bartek told me excitedly that the Home Army needed horses and carts for the Polish evacuation and was offering hard cash for carts recovered from Ukrainian families now trekking eastward. To Polish eyes, this was not theft but the reclaiming of goods looted from Polish villages. Our objective was to stop the goods disappearing forever into the Soviet Union.

I was sceptical at first and I wanted to relax at Sophie's house, but in the end I decided to go off with Bartek. I had already seen the difference in the size of the loads carried by the Polish and Ukrainian carts, and he persuaded me that duty demanded I assist the Polish population.

We rode a couple of borrowed horses to a spot outside the town and waited at the side of the road until two Ukrainians came into sight. They were returning from the east and clearly planned to pick up more possessions, as their wagon was empty and they had no passengers. Not wanting to be recognised, Bartek hid in the bushes, his rifle cocked, as I jumped the startled drivers. I first blasted a shot over their heads and shouted that the next one would be aimed at them if they did not dismount and hand over their vehicle. To confuse them (I was still wearing my Air Force uniform), I spoke Russian in the hope that they would not be able to identify me if ever we came face to face again. I need not have bothered. I don't think they had time to look at me too closely, as they ran off without offering any resistance.

We promptly took the empty cart to a Home Army collecting-point a few miles away, where we were paid in new Polish zlotys. If it had been left up to me, I would then have gone back to my aunt for the rest of Easter, our mission accomplished, but Bartek wanted more and the Home Army sergeant asked us to get another cart.

This time Bartek waited a mile or so outside the town on the same road, which led over the Bug to Wlodizimierz, as I hid on the outskirts of Hrubieszow, intending to hijack a cart and drive it out to him. Pretty soon one came into view, carrying a driver, three women passengers and, as it turned out, several sacks of flour. I waited until it was ten yards away before jumping into the middle of the road and firing a warning shot into the air, as on the previous occasion. I then walked up to them, held my pistol to the head of the youngest woman and shouted to her two companions to get down.

'You've got ten seconds to get on the road, otherwise she gets it.'

The two other women jumped down without arguing. I then switched from Russian to Ukrainian to make sure their male driver understood my instructions. Switching languages would also add to their confusion, or so I hoped, if later they had the chance to report what had happened. I climbed into the back of the cart and told him to get going.

'Don't try anything stupid. I'm aiming right for your kidneys,' I informed him.

He was a typical peasant, stoutly built, with massive, weather-beaten hands, and he showed no signs of undue fear. On the contrary, he smiled and invited me to sit next to him, where it was more comfortable. I declined and he did not bother to ask where we were going or what I intended to do with him, but sped along at a brisk trot. As we reached a narrow stretch of raised road with steep banks on either side, I glimpsed Bartek, pretending to be hitching a lift. At this point the driver suddenly heaved his body to the right, fell from the cart onto the bank and rolled down into the fields and started running, as I half-heartedly fired a shot after him. I had feared that he would try something, thinking perhaps that I was young enough to fall for a trick, but the sight of my companion had probably dissuaded him. Anyway, my pistol jammed after the first shot, as I had loaded it with converted ammunition meant for a different weapon, and he was out of sight before I could get Bartek's gun. We did not mind, however, as the cart was ours and we drove to another collecting point to pick up our reward before returning home for the night.

The next day Bartek persuaded me once more to help him and I agreed, again after some initial reluctance. The money that I had been paid for the first two jobs was enough to live like a king for two whole months, but I also wanted to help my poor compatriots who desperately needed the vehicles. We positioned ourselves nearer the river this time, as the word would undoubtedly have got around that this stretch of road was dangerous. The first Ukrainian cart rolling eastward was loaded high with boxes of sugar – its driver had made off with a good haul.

'Hold it. Hold it now,' I said, as he brought the cart to a halt.

'Now where did you find all that?' I asked with genuine curiosity.

'I bought it from my neighbour,' he replied quite calmly. The boxes had Polish writing on them and bore the name of a Polish merchant. As I was in uniform and still speaking Russian, he had no reason to think that I had been involved in the slaughter of two years ago and knew what had gone on. When he said he had 'bought' the sugar, I simply substituted the word 'stole' in my mind.

'And who was this neighbour of yours?' I continued.

'He was a Polish settler, a friend of mine.'

So, I thought to myself, he admitted the sugar's Polish origin. To me, his story meant that he had made off with the boxes during the general looting and killing.

'If you're telling me lies, I'll have to kill you. We can easily check where it came from,' I threatened.

'I swear I'm telling the truth. He sold me the sugar because he was running away.'

'And who was he running away from?' I wondered silently before letting him go, telling him to run for it over the border and not to venture back into Poland if he valued his life. We accepted no money for this third cart and let the Home Army keep the sugar.

The following day was the last of my leave and I should have been preparing to return to my base. Yet as Bartek wanted to get yet another cart and it had been so easy up till now, I agreed. I thought I was doing something useful to help the Polish survivors obtain at least some redress for the violence of the last few years. Besides, I was enjoying working with him.

'If only I had come back with a machine gun, we could have really cleaned up,' I told Bartek.

The following evening I was driving along the road from Hrubieszow to Wlodizimierz, heading back to the Home Army to hand over the cart, as Bartek lay in the back on some straw, clutching a bottle of home-made vodka and crooning unmelodiously in his drunkenness. Suddenly his singing stopped and, when I turned round to check that he was all right, I saw that he had fallen off the back and lay sprawled on the ground, bottle still in hand. I stopped the horse and lifted him back onto the cart, tossing his bottle of vile-smelling alcohol into a field, and decided to have a rest myself while he slept off some of his stupor. Then I noticed a broken-down cart 200 yards off.

Three figures stood at the roadside. I decided to investigate and, when I drew closer, realised their cart was lurching at an angle into the ditch, one of its rear wheels broken in two.

The cart belonged to a Polish family, mother, father and grown-up daughter, from a town east of the Bug. Their clothes were threadbare and they looked poor and frightened as they stared apprehensively at me, not knowing for sure, as I was still wearing my Soviet uniform, that I was the friend I pretended to be. Their cart contained nothing much except hay and small quantities of grain for their hungry-looking horse. I tried to reassure them by explaining I was a pilot in the Polish Air Force and that they had nothing to fear from me, but they still looked cowed and anxious. The daughter then told me they had been travelling for three days and nights and had covered barely 30 miles, as they had hidden during the day to avoid bandits. I promised that, once we had fixed the wheel, I would accompany them to Hrubieszow, where they would be among Poles.

Before I had time to think how I was going to repair the wheel, a Ukrainian cart came into view. The contrast could not have been greater, which made me furious. The passengers and driver were all well-fed and the cart was laden with household goods. More importantly, two brand new spare wheels hung from either side of it. I drew my pistol.

'Hold it! Get off your wagon, we need one of your wheels.'

The driver had an arrogant, unco-operative expression and at first refused to move. He needed some encouragement.

'If you don't come down, I'll shoot your horses and then I'll shoot you.'

He descended.

'I want you to undo the spare wheel,' I told him, 'so that we can help this Polish man and his family.'

'I need them both for myself,' he answered. 'We have a long way to go. What's it got to do with me if he hasn't brought a spare wheel?'

'If you don't undo it this minute, I might decide to take both of them, as well as one of the other wheels from your wagon and leave you stranded here.'

The Polish family hid behind their cart and the wife, her body shaking with fear, begged me to let them go and not to cause a fight.

'We don't want any more trouble,' she whispered to me. 'We just thank God that we're still alive.'

The Ukrainians might well have had arms hidden in the back of their cart and I had to keep my eye on their every movement.

The Ukrainian eventually did as I asked and unscrewed the wheel. Then he lifted it above his head as if he was about to hurl it to the ground. I had to stop him and told him that he was not finished yet, as I could not have lifted up the cart and fitted the wheel on my own and the Pole was in too much of a state to help. The Ukrainian was built like an ox and had the right equipment to jack up the cart. Bartek slept on, oblivious of what was taking place.

When the Ukrainian had finished his work, I let him back onto his cart and he cracked his whip and sped off as fast as his horse could pull the heavy load. The Polish family thanked me and the woman kissed my hand.

'God bless you,' she said.

I took them to Hrubieszow and then drove the cart and Bartek to the Home Army HQ.

I left Bartek, still barely able to walk after all the vodka he had drunk, at a Polish farm and then returned to Sophie in the town. She saw him the following day in Hrubieszow after I had left for Deblin, but the next time I turned up in Hrubieszow after deserting from the Air Force I learnt that Bartek had vanished. No one had seen him since I left him at the farm and his body was never found. There was little doubt that he had paid with his life for our actions. Sophie wrote to me in London years later that his family still blamed me for his disappearance, as if it had all been my idea.

In the months after the war, Poland sank into lawlessness. Even Home Army soldiers robbed local people they were supposed to be guarding, looted the villages they claimed to be defending and attacked the thousands of Polish workers returning from German factories, who had often left Germany with a few meagre possessions. Any criminal or alcoholic could claim he was a Home Army soldier or a fighter for Free Poland, thereby providing the Soviet authorities with a welcome propaganda gift.

At the end of May, after running away from Deblin, I headed straight for Hrubieszow with the intention of teaming up with another partisan unit. I was back under arms in no time, fighting with a company of the Free Polish Cavalry, all deserters from the Red Polish Army under the command of a pre-war lieutenant. Some of the Home Army refused to disarm when the order came from London and resisted Soviet rule with all the means at their disposal, while avoiding open warfare with the infinitely superior Red Army. We still had faith in the West, which was our last and only hope, as our own units were too small, too scattered and too ill-equipped to contemplate taking on the might of the Red Army, which, now that Germany was defeated, would surely consolidate its grip on the country. But the official Polish militia, the Polish People's Army and the Polish NKVD working with the new Soviet regime took a while to establish their authority. They feared the Poles hiding out in the forests and tended to keep to their fortified stations in the towns and villages.

Our role was now to protect nationalist Poles from the NKVD, who had already imprisoned thousands, while waiting for the Western powers to intervene. It could not be, we reasoned, that the British and Americans would abandon us again after the British had gone to war in the first place because of Poland. Surely, we thought, the West would recognise the valour shown by the Poles in the Battle of Britain, at Tobruk, El Alamein and Monte Cassino. The CO, a very strict, abstemious man, repeated almost daily that he would lay down his arms when General Anders, the Commander in Chief of the free Polish forces in the West, ordered him to do so, and not a moment before.

'Until that order comes, we will fight on regardless of the consequences,' he told his men.

He gave me command of a platoon of machine-gunners,

approximately 50 men, a dozen Spandaus and a couple of Tokarovs. I was now fighting against the side I had served barely two weeks previously.

One sunny afternoon I was sitting in the centre of a village in the east of the Puszcza Solska, talking to a pretty local girl. We had been billeted there for a week or more and I had spoken to her before. She had attended a commercial college during the war and was well spoken. I liked her and it seemed that she liked talking to me, but she was proving a difficult conquest and I was beginning to wonder whether my time and attention were ever likely to bear fruit.

Suddenly the peace was shattered by a bugler charging through the village at full gallop calling the company to arms. We scrambled back to our quarters to fetch horses and weapons, ready for immediate action, and assembled in the village square. The CO explained that he had received emergency orders from the local Home Army commander to ambush a Soviet column on the road to Tomaszow Lubelski that afternoon, where a new regiment of Soviet NKVD and their Polish counterparts had just arrived.

Forty Home Army men, including a major and a lieutenant-colonel with detailed knowledge of the command structure for the whole of the west of the county, had been arrested and were going to be taken under armed escort to the town. We had either to liberate the officers or liquidate them before they could be interrogated. Obviously we hoped to save as many of our compatriots as we could, but the priority was to prevent the NKVD getting its hands on the information.

We loaded twelve Spandau-type machine guns, four water-cooled Maxims and the same number of cannon, capable of firing armour-piercing shells, onto cavalry wagons. If there was no other way, we planned to blow up the whole convoy. After a hard ride we set the ambush 100 yards from the road at a point where woodland gave way to fields of wheat and rye, positioning the Maxim guns and the cannon on the right-hand side, sheltered by the trees. I went to the other side to command two Spandaus hidden in the fields and arranged the positions of the other ten machine guns. The battle plan was simple: after the column had been attacked and immobilised from the right, the NKVD would scramble for cover on the left and prepare to fight it out. Then the Spandaus would mow them down.

I knew from experience that the waiting, whether it lasts five minutes or five hours, is always the worst part of an ambush. We stood ready until dusk and still nothing came. It began to look as if the NKVD had received a tip-off and were taking a different route or holding the men elsewhere. Then, just as it was almost completely dark, we heard the rumble of engines and were able to make out several sets of headlights, three lorries with an armoured car at the front and rear.

Time froze at this point. The tension now threatened to reach breaking point, when nerves would snap and someone would open fire before the order was given, as the convoy crept towards us. It seemed as if it was going to pass without a shot being fired, when suddenly the flare shot into the sky and the cannons blasted at the first armoured car, immobilising it instantly.

Stupidly, all the cannons had fired at the leading armoured car, leaving the other free to switch off its lights and race across the fields on my side of the road to the head of the convoy where it began to answer our fire. As the soldiers poured out of the original leading vehicle, I started shooting as planned, showering the darkness with bullets. I turned to my ammunition supplier to tell him to hold off and realised that he was nowhere to be seen. The other Spandau was abandoned too, and the men must have scarpered to the other side, where they could take cover in the forest.

'The rats,' I thought to myself. 'Wait till I get my hands on them.'

I dived into the fields as the Soviets started to fire at me.

What saved me now was a high bank on either side of the road. The bullets ricocheted off it and failed to hit me. When the gunners turned to face the other way, I took my chance and dashed across in time to follow the retreat signal.

The mission was a success. Half the Home Army men had

scrambled to safety, including the major, but the lieutenant-colonel had been shot by the officer guarding him. The shooting had lasted no more than five minutes and in the end the waiting had been far more painful. Only a couple of our men had bullet wounds. No one was dead on our side, but twenty of the Home Army prisoners had perished, so there could be no celebrating.

Back in the village, I asked to have a word with the CO.

'Is it important?'

'Not very,' I replied.

'Is it to do with the mission?'

'Yes.'

He motioned to me to come in and asked a couple of others to leave. I told him I wanted to get rid of my ammunition supplier. He pressed me for a reason, so I explained.

'He cracked up before the target even got into sight and ran off.'

He did not seem too surprised, or even angry, and asked if I wanted to put in a report and have the man court-martialled. This seemed excessive to me. Here we were, a tiny band of partisans, with no hope of military victory and surely with only a few weeks before we disbanded, and he was suggesting a court martial. What could we do with the fellow? Shoot him for cowardice? What would that achieve? Put him in prison? We had no prison. I replied that I did not think it would be necessary, but that I needed a new ammunition supplier. He agreed.

'As it happens, he's not a bad shot,' the CO said.

'Well, what's the good of that, if he's too scared to shoot?'

He gave me a weary shrug.

I told the man that I had reported him but was not going to press for a court martial. He was ashamed and did not bother to make excuses. In the end I felt sorry for him. I too knew the taste of fear.

I saw as much action in these two months as I did in the Puszcza Solska two years earlier. Like the Peasants' Battalion in the winter of 1943–44, we were constantly on the move and covered much the same territory. The difference for me was that now I had a platoon under me and they called me lieutenant; I was no longer the youngest in the company who had to do the first stint of guard duty each night.

The only skirmish with a Ukrainian unit occurred when we had moved to patrol the border. The CO had ordered me to advance with my platoon to the top of a hill to survey the situation across the Bug. If the coast looked clear, I was to take the lie of the land. The CO wanted a thorough reconnaissance after hearing reports of killings, expecting, if they turned out to be accurate, either the Russian or the Polish NKVD to be responsible. If things grew desperate, he knew he could call on as many as 5,000 men within a 35-mile radius.

I rode on a cart with a Spandau, too heavy to carry on horseback. As we reached the brow of the hill we peered down at the houses and villages stretching into the distance below. It was a beautiful summer's day. The apparently peaceful scene was disturbed by the sight of a large unit of men advancing up to meet us. They were clearly Ukrainians and so I ordered a swift retreat, though I had no way of knowing what they were doing there in such numbers, as we thought they had by now disappeared from the west bank of the Bug. The horses galloped back down the hill as the Ukrainians gave pursuit on foot. My driver took us faster than the terrain allowed, anxious because we brought up the rear and the Ukrainians had started firing, even though they were way out of range. They had no horses and could not possibly catch us; their rifles, let alone tommy guns, could not possibly hit us at that distance.

My driver was a shit-pants who ignored my shouting at him to slow down, and instead charged onwards, as if our lives depended upon it. Before long we hit a tree, the pole snapped in two, the horses continued their gallop in full harness and we were lucky not to get thrown from the cart. But by the time I had picked up the gun and the ammunition box, the driver was 100 yards ahead, sprinting for all he was worth to catch up with the riders, who evidently had not noticed our accident. Unlike him, I considered myself a professional soldier for whom aban-

doning weapons in the field was an offence as serious as cowardice in the face of attack.

I was now in danger. The grassy field soon turned to mud
which clung to my feet like glue, the Spandau became heavier
with every step and my pursuers came closer and closer. They
were firing at me almost continuously but, frightening though
that was, I knew they still had no chance of hitting me. All the
time I prayed that the platoon would notice that I was missing
and see me struggling to catch up. Together, we stood a chance
of taking them on for long enough for me to scramble onto a
horse and be carried to safety.

One of the Ukrainians had broken away from the rest and
was running ahead of them, pausing occasionally to kneel down
and shoot at me. He also fired as he ran, gaining on me with
every stride, though he was still too far off to hit me. Suddenly,
when I was least expecting it, I saw a deep ditch. From there I
could hold them all off, I thought to myself, as my vision would
be perfect. I could spray them all with fire if they approached.
I hurled myself into the ditch and crawled to the far end, where
I had just enough time to put the gun on its biped and load a
belt of bullets. With my first blast I did for the leading
Ukrainian, but I fired at his body for several seconds to make
sure he was not faking. My fear and panic had evaporated in an
instant, giving way to elation, excitement and relief. The
Spandau gave me power, and it was as if my adrenalin pumped
out the ammunition without the help of the firing mechanism.
The rest of the Ukrainians paused to take cover. I had them
pinned down and picked them off as they began to crawl back,
enabling me to make a safe retreat.

In the end we all got back safely and I gave my driver a piece
of my mind. The CO announced that we would have to prepare
to take on the whole Ukrainian unit if Polish families were to be
safe. It turned out, however, that they had been bandits, and
from then on we treated Ukrainians we came across as criminals rather than combat units. We disarmed them and told
them to go back across the river unless they were willing to
entrust their fate to the Polish Communist authorities.

Although, of course, we did not know it at the time, fighting was to continue in the western Ukraine for up to four years. In the Polish Carpathians a handful of Ukrainian nationalists held out into the 1950s, carrying out isolated assassinations and acts of sabotage.

Two days later, as we prepared to move off in pursuit, several Polish refugees passed along the main road. We interviewed them for information about the situation in Galicia and especially Lwow, which they had left a week before. They told us they had been captured by the Ukrainian Nationalist Army, which was fighting the Soviets for an independent Ukraine, and that they had been well treated. They had seen 300 men under arms and had been held by them for a few days but assured that the Ukrainians had nothing against the Poles, that they were fighting the Soviets and that the Poles were their allies. This was strange but welcome news. On release, their captors had advised them where to cross the river into Poland and had even given them food for their journey.

Meanwhile the struggle against the NKVD was intensifying. In June the Home Army command sent word that an NKVD station in the Puszcza Solska was rounding up Home Army sympathisers for torture, imprisonment and execution. The reports were vague – whether it was the NKVD or their newly formed Polish counterparts (the UB) was not stated. After receiving the request to neutralise the Communist strength in this particular village, the CO proceeded cautiously and asked for more information, as was always his way.

After summoning me to see him, the CO got out a map and indicated the village. He did not waste his words.

'You know what to do. Try to get the information without arousing suspicion. If anyone asks what you're doing there, say you're looking for somebody who's gone missing. With any luck you might bump into somebody you recognise who can help you. Whatever you do, be careful and take your time. The lives of the whole unit could depend on what you report.'

I saluted and left his room. A horse had already been saddled for me.

Armed with two grenades strapped to my belt and a pistol in each coat pocket, I rode into the village later that same day after a fifteen-mile journey. I stopped first to ask the inhabitants of a house on the outskirts for water for my horse when I smelt the familiar smell of a vodka distillery. The elderly couple gave me some water and told me that settlers had started up a distillery across the road. Beyond that they proved unforthcoming, so I did not bother to ask them any other questions, deciding instead to investigate the distillery.

I immediately recognised the man who opened the door. Already rather tipsy, he hugged me and invited me in, announcing to the others at the back of the house that an old friend had just showed up out of the blue. That was not strictly true, since the last time I had seen him we had come to blows after drinking too much together. That was safely in the past, however, and now we were friends again: after all the killing, anyone was pleased to see that a familiar face had survived.

'Oh, lieutenant, I see,' he said, after I handed him my coat and he had seen the insignia on my tunic.

'Lieutenant indeed. Congratulations! Come round to the back – we must celebrate. For you, I have a rather special brew. None of this potato stuff,' he said, handing me a glass. 'Corn, pure corn.'

He gestured proudly at his equipment.

I recognised several of the crowd who greeted me and shook their hands. They came mostly from around Mirce and Modryn and had moved to escape the fighting. Others had returned from factories and farms in Germany and found empty houses in the village. Everyone had a tale to tell and we caught up on news of old friends: who had survived and who had not and who was still missing. Conversation then turned to the future. The mood was celebratory, the girls giggled as they drank and the men fell to the ground, slapping their thighs.

'Drink, drink! I've got a whole barrel of the stuff,' my host repeated each time he came round with a bottle.

In the end, all I could do was to tip it away while no one was looking. Even so, I got pretty drunk.

I asked my host why he had not joined the partisans, as I had done, and he gave the usual explanation. Others nodded as he spoke.

'I had a mother and three sisters to think about. We're not all as hot-headed as you. When we saw signs of trouble we moved here. Nothing is left of Mirce now. We'd have been dead if we hadn't come here. The Nazis took everyone to work in the Reich or carted them off to the camps. Anyone still alive has moved here.'

I knew this to be true from what Sophie had told me in Hrubieszow. The population of Mirce moved 50 miles west to take over abandoned houses, although a few peruple trickled back later.

I knew that he and his friends were not Communists and began to ask them about the NKVD station in the village and found out everything I needed to know in a matter of minutes. No one had heard of any special operations against the Home Army or any other Poles, whether under arms or not. That was reassuring, but I would still have to check. Unfortunately, by dusk I had drunk rather more than I planned and, encouraged by the apparent success of my mission and the convivial company, responded to what I took to be the advances of the girl sitting opposite me.

'Shall we go outside for a walk?' I asked. 'I need to clear my head.'

She agreed and we went for a stroll down the main street. I put my arm round her and she kissed me, letting me stroke her body in the darkness behind some trees. But by the time we had reached her house, she had changed her mind and wanted to go inside. I felt offended that she did not want me. I took off my coat to show her how we could lie together in a field at the back and enjoy the warm summer night. She pushed me away, but I was in no mood to take no for an answer and pushed her up against the gate. Then she screamed. Unfortunately I had failed to notice that her house stood next to the NKVD station.

A man in civilian clothes rushed out of the station, followed by a junior sergeant from the Polish arm of the NKVD. Perhaps she had brought me there on purpose. My coat hung around both our shoulders as she struggled to escape. A woman, who turned out to be the girl's mother, stood behind the two NKVD men, shouting abuse at me. Releasing the girl, I lunged inside my coat and pulled out a grenade.

'If you don't put down that rifle, I'm going to throw this into the house,' I threatened.

The woman calmed down and tried to reason with me.

'Please leave my daughter alone. She's a good girl. She's engaged to be married – she can't go off with you, lieutenant.'

'I wasn't holding her against her will. A few moments ago she was perfectly willing. Now I've brought her home. I don't know why she screamed. Everything's all right.'

I then opened the gate for her to pass through and turned to leave.

A few seconds later I felt an almighty blow to the head and collapsed to the ground. The blows showered down on me, aimed at my face and head, which I protected as best I could with my hands and arms. Each blow felt like an explosion as it hit my skull, stinging without drawing blood. Time after time the NKVD pair took turns to beat me, while a third occasionally directed a well-aimed kick at my stomach. The beating went on and on as I groaned and yelled, struggling to avoid the shower of blows. Finally, they began to question me.

'What are you doing here? What did you do to the girl? Who sent you here?'

Then one of the NKVD men recognised the Air Force insignia on my shoulder, which, in their haste to inflict pain, neither had noticed before.

'Have you deserted?' the sergeant yelled at me. Then, turning round to the others gathered in front of the station, 'Hey, we've got a deserter. This one's a lieutenant in the Air Force. Where's your unit, lieutenant?'

I managed to mutter that I was on leave.

'And so where is your leave slip then, sir?'

He pronounced the last word with all the sarcasm of a frustrated NCO who at last found himself in a position to hit back at an officer.

One of them held me while the sergeant went through my pockets where he found the other grenade and the two pistols.

'Do you always go on holiday with two hand-grenades and a couple of pistols in your pockets? Are you trying to make idiots out of us? Because if you are, then I'm warning you. I've never known an airman who goes on leave as heavily armed as you.'

I tried to tell him that as an officer I was allowed to carry a pistol while off-duty, even when on leave. Then the blows started once more, each aimed at my head and face which I again did my best to cover with my arms.

'We've got plenty of time,' the sergeant assured me. 'You'll pass out long before we get tired. And then we'll have to revive you – it's all right, we're used to that in this job. And if you still don't tell us what you're doing here, then we have a cellar inside the building where nobody can hear you scream, no matter how loud you holler.'

He said this slowly in his dreadful sneer. I had not been aware that I had been screaming, but I suppose half the village must have heard me. I could no longer see, but I could tell that lights were on and had the impression that I was at the centre of a small crowd of spectators. 'If we take you to the cellar, we can chop off your balls and no one will hear so much as a murmur.'

He whispered the last sentence directly into my ear. I wanted to tell them they were just like the Nazi swine who had beaten me up in the past, but I had had enough and I just wanted it to stop. I confessed that I had been sent to investigate their crimes against patriotic Poles, reasoning that they must know all about the cavalry company since it had recently passed through several nearby villages. Still they asked what cavalry I was talking about.

'You know what cavalry,' I muttered.

They stopped hitting me and I continued.

'They sent me to find out … The CO had reports. Twenty-five local men executed. I have to find out and then report.'

Two of them propped me up so that I could talk better. They seemed to have lost their nerve as their tone had changed.

'Who told you we had done that?'

'There were reports, independent reports,' I mumbled. They did not deny anything or make any comment.

'And what are you going to say when you get back?'

'I haven't had time to get anything. You didn't give me any time. I only arrived this afternoon. I didn't have a chance. I was only obeying the orders of my commanding officer.'

'Who is your commanding officer?' one demanded.

'He's a colonel,' I lied. 'I can't give you his name.'

'Are you under his direct orders?'

'Yes.'

I knew what the next question was going to be.

'And what is the strength of the unit?'

'One thousand men, plus auxiliaries. It's a full battalion. That's why he's a colonel.' He would have expected me to exaggerate, but not, I hoped, by that much. I wanted to confuse them.

'And where is this battalion?'

'Not far from here.'

'What's your rank? Why did they send you?'

'Battalion adjutant.'

Now the sergeant, who had done most of the beating but had subsequently gone rather quiet, found his voice again.

'Aren't you rather young to be an adjutant?'

He still had the sneer, but was no longer quite so confident.

'The colonel ordered me and I didn't argue. Why does age matter? I carry out my duties to the best of my ability and that's why I'm here.'

'What does your colonel plan to do?'

'That depends on me. If I don't come back within three days he'll assume that you've finished me off, like you did the others. Then he'll come to get you.'

The sergeant ran inside the station to wake up a superior, but none of them would come out. They did not want me to be able to recognise them later. He returned and asked almost politely where I was sleeping that night and then sent a corporal to the house where I had left my horse to fetch three or four men to carry me home. They had to drape my arms over their shoulders and drag me back up the road.

After a fitful sleep, I could not see when I tried to open my puffed-up eyes the next morning. My face and head had swollen too, my ears looked like balloons, my lips were lacerated and my arms had turned black and blue from taking the full force of so many blows. Even breathing caused me great pain. They must have been using rubber truncheons to cause maximum discomfort but leave only severe bruising afterwards. If they had been hitting me with wooden clubs, my skull would have been split open.

A couple of girls cleaned me up and bathed my eyes so that I could partially open them after an hour or so. They put a straw in my mouth and told me to suck the sugary milk they had made for me. I stayed with them for five days, until I was fit enough to ride on the back of a cart and return to my unit. In the meantime the sergeant turned up with my pistols and grenades and apologised for the beating.

'Why didn't you tell us you were in the Air Force? If you'd identified yourself at the beginning we would never have hit you.'

He did not mention anything about the cavalry, but implied that I had been forced into the role of scout and was really still an officer in the Air Force. That way he saved face, I suppose. He knew that the Home Army had men under arms, that he was in an exposed area and could expect me to single him out if we returned. He still did not mention the allegations and indicated I would be free to go where I pleased when I had recovered. After he had gone, I had a stream of other visitors, none of whom had heard of any atrocities committed by the NKVD in the village. The reports must have been fabricated. The one fatality which several people told me about concerned a robber in Home Army uniform who had been shot for holding up returnees from the German factories. The militia had shot him when he refused to surrender. I could only conclude that his case had provided the basis for the rumours and returned to report to my CO a week after leaving on my ill-fated mission.

Not long afterwards, just before we disbanded and went our separate ways, we passed through a village on the border where the locals had not seen Polish troops before and were still petrified of the Ukrainians. It was a Sunday and everyone was celebrating some sort of summer festival. We heard music as we approached. When the people saw us, they stopped their dancing, the band struck up the Polish anthem and the crowds parted to the edge of the road to cheer us into their village.

'Bravo! God bless you! Good luck!' they shouted. Old women went down on their knees and wept and I began to think I had just helped liberate my country. We must have made an imposing sight, 100 marching men, 50 more on horseback with the carts carrying supplies bringing up the rear, all of us in uniform emblazoned with the Polish eagle. In order to show off, I had my machine gun with bipeds open ready for action over my shoulder and felt like the conquering hero.

We also visited the village where I had received my hiding and interrupted another village party. The CO wanted to show the local people that we were still there and that the cause was not lost, as well as demonstrating to the NKVD that they had no chance of taking us on. We had cut the telephone lines before we entered the village and were ready to jump to our positions if they opened fire. They did not do so and we marched directly to the station where I had suffered the beating a month before. The sergeant saw me and dashed inside. There was not an officer in sight. The CO walked up and took out a loud-hailer so that the whole village as well as those inside the NKVD building could hear him.

'We have a reason to be here and wish to stay for the festivities. We don't intend to attack you but we will respond in kind if you make a move against us.'

They sent out a Polish captain who told us we were welcome to stay as long as we liked and should join in the dancing if we wanted. Thirty of us stood behind the CO, fully armed with grenades, pistols and machine guns. The rest had already started to drink and make merry with the villagers. We were their friends; the enemy was within the fortified walls of the NKVD station. I asked a private to hold my gun while I danced with a girl. I was the happy young officer again and I danced and drank until midnight, when the company moved on to more cheers and clapping from the crowd.

That triumphant entrance and departure proved to be our last great fling. Perhaps the CO knew already that our days as a company were now numbered. Soviet divisions were on the move back through Poland, some to bases and demobilisation centres in the Soviet Union, others to garrisons in other parts of the country. We had no chance against the Red Army. Many in the company had served in the pre-war Polish forces, then suffered deportation to Soviet labour camps in 1939–40 before joining the Red Polish Army, only to desert from it once the war against Germany was over. They knew what the Soviet Union was all about.

The CO took me to a meeting of the regional Home Army command to hear a colonel under instructions from the Government in Exile. He was an imposing figure, well-informed and a good speaker, used to taking charge and making an impression. I imagined that he had been an agent for the Allies during the war and stayed on to work for the West now that the war had ended. He seemed to have a complete overview of the situation and spoke as if London was his second home. He did not tell us that the government had ordered us to lay down our arms but instead appealed to our common sense.

'The West is not going to come to our aid,' he intoned, and for the first time I realised that he must be right. 'But as long as the unrest in Poland continues, and until the Communist government is able to organise and to identify all its new citizens, we stand a chance of escaping. The local command can issue all our men with new identities and new papers. The best chance for them is to take these new papers and resettle in the recovered territories where they won't be known.'

My CO argued against the plan and said what he had repeated to his men on so many occasions. 'We must wait for orders from General Anders before we give up the fight. He is our Commander in Chief. We take our orders from him. He must have reasons for us to continue.'

'How long can you hold out against a Soviet division?' the colonel asked him. Not very long, was the reluctant reply.

'That is precisely my point. If we carry on fighting, they'll catch us like rats, one by one.'

Someone asked how our safety could be guaranteed by assuming new identities and where we could get so many forged papers.

'The local command can pass on the details of the practical arrangements to you. It has worked on a smaller scale in the past. I see no reason for it not to succeed again now. How many are in favour?'

Only about half of us raised our hands.

We got back from the meeting and the next morning the whole company was resigned to what was going to happen. Many of them were on NKVD lists, as I was, and had to be careful. A photographer took our pictures and within two days we had new documents with false names and false dates of birth. I chose the name Henrik Korycki and decided on 1926 as my year of birth. The years 1924–25 were best avoided as these were now liable for military service. Any NKVD officer who stopped a man of that age had the power to put him straight into the army. 1923 would have made me twenty-two and I still barely had a beard, so thought it best to pretend to be younger rather than older. I had no intention of still being in the country for the next recruitment the following year. We were also given money, told to sell our horses to local people and to hand in our weapons. I discovered I was more attached to my machine gun than to my horse and I kissed it farewell. If no one had been looking I might even have shed a tear for it – after all, it had saved my life more than once.

Everyone pored over maps of the new territories, resigned to their futures rather than excited by them. It seemed to be everyone's intention to find a nice girl and settle down to farm some land. I announced that I was heading off to find the free

Polish forces in the West as I still dreamed of joining the air force. The women in the village where we were staying cried as they saw us preparing to depart. They helped us into civilian clothes and gave us food. The college girl I had been courting still refused to spend the night with me but asked me to write to her. She said she was not interested in a one-night stand, that she wanted a man for her whole life. I told her I would come back with the British and Americans.

'And when I return, I'll do a roll in my Spitfire over the village and dip my wings three times so that you know it's me.'

10

Escape To the West, July 1945

My first thought was to get back to Zakzrouvek to see my family and talk to friends of my cousins with underground contacts. I no longer had anything in common with them politically, as they stuck to the views of the pre-war ruling elite of nationalists, aristocrats and the military. But it was possible they would be able to tell me of a route to reach the West through Germany, where the borders between the Soviet and Western zones of occupation were beginning to harden.

Travelling alone was dangerous and the new authorities were on the look-out for anti-Communist saboteurs and ex-Nazis. I guessed it would be safer to avoid Lublin and Zamosc, which, together with the erratic train service, still interrupted where the bombed or dynamited tracks had not been repaired, made for an arduous journey. The trains were full of Red Army troops and Polish workers still making their way home from the Reich. I was lucky to be asked for my new papers only once.

At one small station I jumped off the roof of the wagon to run to the toilets. As there were none I was obliged to go round to the back of the station building to relieve myself. An NKVD captain spotted me as I re-emerged.

'Stop!' he shouted and indicated to me with his gun to come closer.

'Keep your hands away from your pockets, young man.'

When I was standing opposite him, he looked me up and down and fixed his eyes for a few seconds on my Russian boots.

They were a good pair and I had purposefully kept them for what I knew would be a long trek.

'So, you got scared when you saw me and tried to run away. That may have serious consequences for you. You can't evade the police for long.'

'I was dying for a piss, captain,' I answered, aware of my cheekiness but confident my cover was adequate.

'You can use polite language when you're talking to a Russian officer! You're a deserter, anyone can see that.'

'I have my papers with me. You can even come and see that I relieved myself. I couldn't hold it – I'll show you. Here are my papers.'

'Why didn't you go between the wagons?' he asked.

'The Poles are eccentric people,' I explained with foolish disrespect. 'They don't like to piss in front of others.'

This time he did not react but merely gestured for me to hand over my papers. He remarked that I looked older than nineteen and then asked where my boots came from.

'I bought them from a Red Army soldier who was selling off lots of pairs,' I replied.

'And what were you wearing before?'

This was standard NKVD questioning. Always try to make the suspect contradict himself or watch him hesitate.

'I had a flimsy pair of Polish plimsolls which were useless. I knew that Soviet boots would last at least two winters, if not longer.'

This was my old ploy: say anything you can in praise of the Soviet Union, socialism or Stalin, even if it's only in favour of a pair of second-hand boots, and the NKVD will not contradict you. If I had praised the Red Army's boots, how could he accuse me of desertion? Luckily, he did not notice that I was also wearing a Soviet-made shirt.

'Do you realise you'll be drafted into the new Polish army very shortly?'

'I want to go now, but they told me I had to wait another year,' I answered with as much conviction as I could muster.

He let me continue on my journey.

For the last stretch of the way I got a lift in a Red Army lorry. To save petrol it was being towed by another lorry and the driver of the first one told me to keep his colleague awake by talking to him. They had been driving for a day and a half without a rest.

I looked forward to a few days' rest and some decent food in Zakzrouvek before setting out once more, but my family's mood was uneasy, to say the least, as they knew they stood to lose everything they owned and feared worse than that. My father's eldest brother, now approaching seventy, had just returned from Soviet captivity, his health and spirit broken. Yet, as it turned out, the lands and the property would not be confiscated for another year, and meanwhile everything continued to function more or less as of old. A few years later my mother and father, by then in their fifties, would apply for manual jobs in the state-owned mill which used to belong to us and be turned down. My cousin's husband, who had taken over the day-to-day management of the mill and the dam, would be sent to Siberia and the remaining family, my parents and brother and sister included, would destroy all evidence that they had led bourgeois lives in the previous epoch. My younger brother was to spend 104 days on death row for the murder of an NKVD official. In the end he was reprieved on the grounds that, at the age of seventeen, he was too young to be shot. He was released from prison in 1956 during the Khrushchev thaw, but his health had been ruined and he eventually died in an institution in 1982. Our mother died peacefully in her bed at Christmas ten years later; I last saw her at my son's wedding in London in the early 1980s. But history reached out to get my father. Officially, the cause of his death in 1960 was suicide, but Uncle Stanislaw, the born survivor who had joined the Party, hinted to me that old enemies had settled a score by bumping him off. He was afraid to put what he knew in writing, but Pilsudski's ex-legionaries were hardly honoured veterans in the new Poland. Stanislaw was to die by his own hand in the late 1970s after falling ill with cancer; he hanged himself when the pain became more than he could bear. Only Edek, Sophie and my sister are still alive. I have never been back to see them.

Two months after the end of the war the fighting had not stopped around Zakzrouvek any more than it had in the Puszcza Solska. While the Home Army had been thin on the ground locally during the German occupation, it had been the Polish Communists under a certain Major Cien who had taken the war to the Nazis. As there had been no Ukrainian threat, they had concentrated on sabotage and lost countless men and women. Cien took over the administration and policing in the south of the county of Lublin after the liberation and now pursued right-wing Poles ruthlessly, deporting nationalists and Home Army sympathisers wherever he caught them. He had particular reason to hate them because, when the Germans had surrounded his company in the spring of 1944, the nationalists had not come to his aid, clearly hoping that the Nazis would finish him off. He had not forgotten this and neither had the Home Army resigned itself to his control. What made it worse for me was that Cien knew of my cousins' sympathies and had installed a militia contingent in a building on my family's estate, 100 yards from the mill.

I arrived home on a hot summer's evening. My cousins and family were pleased to see me, happy I was still alive, but reluctant to hear my news. They seemed happier not to know what I had been up to and perhaps it was better that way. I was the wild boy in their eyes, a law unto himself who would surely land them all in trouble. I learnt some fifteen years later that people in the village still blamed me for the bloodbath which took place that same evening.

Shortly after six o'clock I was sitting on the far side of the dam from the heavily fortified militia station with two of my younger cousins, enjoying the evening sun. Earlier in the day we had heard screams after two men had been bundled into the building. The screams had now stopped and the scene was peaceful until three lorries drew up and unloaded a group of Home Army soldiers armed with grenades and heavy machine guns.

'Throw out your arms and surrender!' the Home Army leader shouted. The station was protected by a thick steel door and wire netting over the windows to repel hand-grenades. It was impregnable to any force without armour-piercing shells. My cousins were shaking with fear when the shooting started and I made them shelter behind the mill as we listened to the gunfire. I was determined to watch from a safe distance, and peered round the corner of the building. There seemed to me no way that the attackers could break into the building, but after grenades and machine guns had failed, one of the Home Army men crawled to the door, deposited something which must have been an anti-tank device and scurried back down the bank as the others created mayhem to cover his movements. Seconds later an explosion ripped through the steel door and knocked out a corner of the wall. The soldiers sprayed machine-gun bullets through the gaping hole before storming inside.

After the shooting had stopped and the trucks had sped off, I walked towards the smouldering entrance and stepped inside to find sixteen bodies, all Polish NKVD men, sprawled where they had fallen, killed either by the blast or the machine-gun fire. Desks and filing cabinets were peppered with bullet holes and the floor was covered in blood. The raiders had taken arms, ammunition and documents and rescued the two prisoners from the cellar. The raid was highly professional and had been a complete success. What sickened me was that Poles now killed Poles with such casual efficiency.

I then raced back to my parents' house on the other side of the mill. They had heard all the shooting.

'Dirty sods,' my father said. 'Those boys had all fought the Nazis. I know their families. What good will it do to mow down fellow Poles like that?'

'I'm going West,' I announced. 'If they catch me here, I'll be for it.'

My mother looked sad but she did not cry. As she prepared some bread for me, we heard a dozen trucks pull up. Then a voice cried out, 'Major Cien! Don't shoot.'

I raced outside to get a glimpse of what was happening. One of the two soldiers who entered the station staggered back outside and was sick. Some people from the village came to tell them what had happened and ten of the trucks then sped off in the direction of the forests where the raiders had disappeared. Cien would now want his revenge.

My mother handed me a satchel with food. I kissed her on the cheek and then, following the Polish custom, kissed my father on the hand and jumped out of the back window to slip away to the nearest station. It was the last time I saw my father. I rode on the roof of a train headed for Krasnik, the last place I wanted to be, as Cien had his HQ there, and jumped off as we passed through some empty fields. I felt lucky to be alive as I fell asleep in a haystack that night.

I knew where I was going and wanted to get there as quickly as I could. Altogether the 600-mile journey to the new inter-German border took me a fortnight. I lived off unripe fruit picked from trees at the wayside and carrots I found growing in the fields. It was summer, the weather was good and I spent the nights under the stars. For some of the way I careered along dirt tracks on a stolen bicycle, but in the main I hitched lifts on Polish carts or sometimes with military lorries. If I was stopped by a Soviet officer, I planned to say that I wanted to settle in Silesia where my family had already found a farm. Thousands of people were on the road for the same reason, mostly on foot, lugging their belongings behind them on little carts.

The trains were full of Red Army troops or, generally in different wagons, Polish civilians, either seeking their fortune in the new territories or moving back to their pre-war homes. Travelling was dangerous for everybody and safety was in numbers, as bandits and robbers picked off the unwary or the unlucky. Soviet troops faced punishment for rape or robbery, but were not above either, especially when drunk. The most pitiful travellers I passed were a group of *Volksdeutsche* being shepherded onto a train to Germany. They looked even poorer than the Poles heading for Silesia, fear showed in their expressions and their eyes seemed full of sadness. Under Soviet escort, the Poles could not bother them, but others, especially Poles who had germanised their names for personal advantage during the Nazi occupation, met with rough justice all over the country.

Once in Silesia, more than half-way to Germany, a Polish family stopped to pick me up in their cart. They were a couple in their forties with a teenage daughter who was too shy to talk to me. They had with them a plough and other pieces of agricultural equipment and told me they already had a new home allocated to them. They had travelled from the western Ukraine where the father had gone originally to make a living after the First World War. I asked him where they had lived and he said Bielo Kranitza, a village near Kremenets. He had been a caretaker in the castle. It seemed strange that we had never come across one another, as there had been so few Poles in the neighbourhood. But it turned out we had common acquaintances and that his daughter had gone to my school, but as she was two years younger than me I did not remember her. I asked him how Kremenets had fared when the Red Army moved in and it seemed from what he said that the mountains had protected the town from bombardment and the Germans had not bothered to defend it. He was not sorry to be leaving and hoped for a better life in Silesia.

He took a fatherly interest in me and generously shared the family's provisions. The following morning he seemed lost in thought and obviously had something on his mind. Then he began to speak.

'Listen, why take a chance by going to the West? You don't know what lies in store for you over there. I've met dozens of people coming back from Germany and they all say the same. It's even worse over there than it is here. There are thousands of people of all nationalities in Displaced Persons camps with nothing to eat. Why don't you come with us? We could do with the help and you seem like a well brought-up boy. You'd have my daughter for company. She's intelligent and she carried on studying right through the war. She would make any young fellow a good wife and she speaks Russian, which might come in useful nowadays. She's even quite a good cook.'

I was not sure what to say. His daughter had hidden her face in the back of the wagon and pretended not to hear what her father was talking about. I did not want to offend them after their hospitality, so I told them the truth.

'It would be an honour to get to know your daughter and settle down with you, but I'm afraid that I would only bring trouble. I deserted from the Air Force and I've fought with the partisans against the Reds. The NKVD have all my details and would get me in the end – that's why I have to go West.'

He accepted this and wished me luck when we parted company at the end of the day.

That night, after walking along a narrow track for several miles, I went up to a prosperous-looking farmhouse. I asked the woman who opened the door for a piece of bread or a potato, offering money in return. She refused to accept any payment and instead invited me inside where she sat me down to a cooked meal, the first proper food I had eaten in more than a week. When she asked me where I came from and why I was travelling, I asked where she was from rather than giving her a direct answer. Once she had told me that she had fled the county of Volhynia in 1943 to escape the Ukrainian onslaught and had lost her husband in the fighting, I felt safe to say I wanted to go to the West, though I did not feel any need to explain why. I appreciated her food and the comfortable surroundings, but there was no reason for me to confide in her. She told me she had stayed in a house in the Polish city of Bialystok until the war ended and then moved to Silesia on her own when she saw announcements in the newspapers promising land and property to new settlers. She hoped to re-marry and farm the land, starting her life all over again.

By then it was getting late and she offered me a bed for the night.

'My boyfriend won't mind,' she said. 'He's all right, but don't tell him you want to go to the West. Just say you're looking for a place to set up home, like everybody else. I'll explain that we know each other from Volhynia.'

This was the first I had heard about her boyfriend and the thought of a male presence in the house made me uneasy.

'Won't he be jealous if he finds me here?' I asked.

'Oh, he trusts me, and besides you're rather young for my taste,' she said with a grin. 'Do you speak Russian?'

When she had said that she had a boyfriend, I had assumed he was a Pole. Now it turned out she was living with a Red Army NCO.

A few minutes later a Russian staff sergeant let himself into the kitchen and, true to her word, she introduced me as an old acquaintance.

'That's an occasion to celebrate,' he said and placed a bottle of vodka on the table. He was a pleasant fellow and I immediately took to him. My hostess sipped a single glass while the two of us polished off the bottle together. He was genuinely friendly and invited me to stay for a few days while I looked round for the sort of house I wanted.

'There are plenty of 'em,' he said. 'The Germans have all cleared off. Take your time and keep her company in the meantime. She gets bored. She's a good woman, though.'

With that he gave her a cheerful slap on the backside and the two of them disappeared to bed, leaving me to curl up on the couch.

He left early the next morning, before I was up, but his girlfriend's attitude to me had changed completely as she gave me breakfast. She began to apologise for living with a Russian soldier, obviously thinking that I must find it distasteful or unpatriotic, despite the quantities of vodka I had shared with him the previous evening. As a single woman, she explained, she needed help to get herself back on her feet.

'In war women have to do things they wouldn't dream of doing in peacetime. We all have to survive. He wouldn't have done anything to you, even if you'd told him where you were going. He'd do the same if he could, but I think he's got a family back in Russia. He can't leave them.'

I found it very odd that someone who had put me up and given me food should make excuses. I did not say that I had done things which were far worse. She gave me milk and cake for breakfast and wrapped up bread, cheese and cucumber in newspaper for my journey. When we parted, I kissed her hand and could see a tear in her eye. As I walked away I reflected that if she had felt guilty for receiving help from a Russian, then what did that make me, who had accepted her hospitality?

The next day I reached the new German border and peered back from a hilltop in the direction of Poland. It was to be the last time I would set eyes on my native country. The gentle valleys looked very beautiful in the summer sun and gave no hint that all around people were suffering. But Germany itself was in far worse condition than Poland. There was nothing to eat in the fields, not even root vegetables to grub up, and everywhere I looked I saw signs of the fighting, which had ceased only about three months earlier. Nothing had been planted in the spring, which meant there was to be no harvest in the autumn. There were very few men between the ages of sixteen and fifty to be seen; most of the women between those ages had been raped by Soviet soldiers, who had been permitted to do whatever they liked in German territory. The only way for the surviving women to look after their children was to sleep with the soldiers. The roads were choked with troops moving in all directions, Germans and *Volksdeutsche* from the lost provinces in Poland trekking into Germany, and Polish and Russian civilians returning from the factories in the Ruhr. It crossed my mind that Uncle Edek was still making his way back, as my mother had heard that he had survived.

Once in Germany I threw away my forged identity papers and decided I would tell any NKVD or Red Army soldier who stopped me that I had been a forced labourer in the Reich and was now going back home. If they asked why I was headed in the wrong direction, I would just say I had got lost. If they found me with wartime Polish ID, they would think I was a deserter or, worse, a war criminal fleeing justice.

I was lucky that it took me only three days to reach the border town of Plauen in the Thuringian forests. But there I ran into the police and was forced to follow a handful of people to a large farm where more than 100 refugees from Poland, Latvia, Lithuania and the Ukraine were crowded into the out-buildings and stables. I became friendly with two girls from Latvia who had left their homes five months earlier, hoping to reach America. They wanted to come with me on a dash across the border, but I thought they would be a liability and told them that pretty young girls could always find ways of getting across the border without putting themselves in danger. If they came with me, they could easily get fired on. This did not seem to bother them, but still I refused. I waited in the stables throughout the following day, thinking I might make a run for it the following evening under dark.

An hour before dusk a Red Army truck drew up and everyone was ordered outside. They lined us up and inspected our papers. Some of the Latvians and Lithuanians, though not the two girls, were immediately put in the truck. Others were told to wait against a wall. The Soviets would assume that anyone from either country trying to get to the West was a Nazi collaborator, perhaps even an SS veteran. When my turn came, the sergeant barked for my papers.

'I don't have any,' I answered in Russian. 'I've been working in a factory in Frankfurt and I'm trying to get home.'

'Don't you know there are transit camps for people like you? You have to go to a camp first and get ID.'

'Yes I know. But I was waiting for three months in a camp near Frankfurt – the bureaucracy takes ages. I thought they didn't want me to get back to my family in Poland. That's why I left to make my own way.'

'What do you mean, you've got family in Poland? You're not Polish – you come from western Russia. You're Russian.'

I explained that I used to live in the Ukraine but that my family had now moved west, as far as I knew, and that I was Polish.

'Don't you know that Poland's borders have changed?' I asked him, assuming the tone of an ex-lieutenant addressing an NCO. 'Comrade Stalin has declared that all Poles must live in their own land. They don't want me in the Soviet Union. I'm Polish and I want to go back to Poland.'

The Russians' attitude changed whenever Stalin's name was mentioned. To argue with me now would have involved a risk of contradicting Comrade Stalin. He then told me how to find the nearest transit camp where I could be issued with provisional ID and then wait for a train to take me home. That was kind of him because I knew where to avoid. I set off in the late evening and walked a couple of miles in the direction he had indicated before turning back on my tracks.

Altogether Soviet troops stopped me four more times before I crossed into the West. The next occasion was a day later as I was walking through a wood roughly parallel to what I thought must be the border. Three soldiers jumped out onto the track 100 yards ahead of me.

'Halt!' one of them yelled and opened fire with his tommy gun as I turned to run. I dived into the trees and crawled along in the undergrowth as he loosed off a few more rounds. I had nothing whatsoever to eat, no map and no compass and only my sense of direction to tell me where I might succeed in crossing. There were no signposts, not even markers in the ground or wire to indicate the border. After a night in the wood I emerged from a thick concentration of trees and almost fell into a Soviet encampment. This time there was no point in trying to run away.

An NCO carefully cocked his rifle and aimed it at my head from a distance of ten feet. I looked up at him as he ordered me to put my hands up.

'Who are you then, a spy?' he shouted. 'Show me your papers!'

A young captain listened a few paces away while I was interrogated. When the NCO had finished, he turned to the captain, who now came towards us.

'Aha,' he said. 'Another deserter. There seem to be a lot of you about at the moment.'

He was young for a captain, possibly only a year older than me, but his chest was covered in decorations and medals, including the Order of Lenin. He was obviously no coward and had the look of a dedicated Party member. He looked me up and down and walked around me before he spoke again.

'You're clearly a deserter from the Soviet armed forces. You can't possibly have come from the American zone, as you've just claimed. You're trying to escape there. That seems far more likely to me than the fairy story you've just been telling us.'

'First of all, I'm not Russian,' I stammered. 'I'm Polish.'

'Never mind trying to tell me you're a Pole,' he bawled into my ear. 'I can tell from your accent that you're Russian. I've just marched the whole way through Poland with the Red Army. I know exactly how Poles speak Russian. What do you think I am? An idiot?'

I did not try to contradict him as he was in full flow. He had a nasty voice and I feared he would not be as ready as my previous Soviet questioners to let me go.

'Do you know that I have the authority to shoot deserters on the spot?' He pulled out his gun. He was serious and I was much too scared to talk.

'If you tell me the truth, you might get away with a year in Siberia.'

He then quizzed me on which battalion and which division of the Red Army I had been in and I continued to deny everything. Fear of what he might do to me had paralysed my brain and I could think of no way out or anything which I might say to convince him.

'Lies aren't going to save you,' he shouted in the way a sergeant major shouts at a recalcitrant recruit.

'You should know by your age that the Party punishes traitors and deserters, just as it punishes collaborators and Hitlerites.'

That last word was the one that saved me. As soon as he had called me a Hitlerite, my temper snapped and I knew what to say.

'You have no right to call me a Nazi!' I roared back at him. 'We were fighting the Nazis two years before you even joined the war. I was in the forest fighting the Germans before I was caught and sent to do forced labour. I'm not a Nazi. I've just got away from the filthy bastards.'

He was taken aback and seemed ready to listen to what I said.
'As a Polish Communist I thought that the Party rewarded people who fight for their country and take up arms against oppressors. I'm trying to get away from the West. I don't want to be brainwashed by capitalists. I want to get back to free democratic Poland, which has now been liberated by the greatest man on earth, Comrade Stalin. I was a member of the Polish Communist Party, which has now formed the government in the new Poland with the help of the Red Army. How can you accuse me of collaborating with the Nazis?'

I blurted all this out without really thinking what I was saying, so deep was my anger, but I had said it all in a loud enough voice for the NCOs and privates to hear. Its effect was instantaneous, and he stopped threatening me. I knew that no Party member felt absolutely secure in his position and that a false move could cost him his job, his status, even his life. Doubts crept into his expression and after a pause he asked what, as a loyal Party member, I would do if I were in his shoes. I replied that the first thing I would do would be to establish whether or not the suspect was telling the truth.

'And how would you go about this task, comrade?'

The last word clearly stuck in his throat.

'I would find a Polish Communist officer or Party member,' I replied more calmly than before. 'And I would ask him to conduct an interrogation with the aim of finding out whether or not the suspect is Polish as he claims to be and which part of Poland he comes from.'

Suddenly it was as if we were talking officer to officer. Before my outburst showing him my knowledge of Comrade Stalin he had thought I was a peasant.

He had no answer and ordered a warrant officer to put me under guard in a barn. Then he disappeared to let me sweat. After an hour's rest on the straw I persuaded the guard to bring me some food, saying that the captain had allowed it. In the end he even gave me a second helping of gruel and potatoes and a ration of tinned backfat. With a full belly I lay down and waited, unsure what would happen to me next. In the evening the captain returned with a Polish corporal, a shrewd questioner who asked about things which only pre-war Polish schools would have taught. He assured the captain that I was Polish, as I claimed, and had obviously attended a Polish school.

'You see all the trouble I've gone to on your behalf? You're a lucky man. Other officers in my position would have had you shot before they asked any questions.'

I thanked him and asked him whether he would let me continue my journey to Poland. He then directed the warrant officer to draw me a map to help me find the nearest transit camp. As I left them I thought it wise to travel several miles in the right direction before heading back south for the border. I could not afford another encounter like that.

A couple of hours later I bumped into a fellow of about my age and asked him in halting German where we were. He asked what nationality I was and, on hearing my answer, started to talk in fluent Polish. He told me he came from a Polish-German family in Silesia and that the Nazis had conscripted him into the Wehrmacht. At the end of the war he had ended up in a Displaced Persons camp in the American zone from where he had made his way home, only to find that his family had disappeared and his village had been devastated. Now he wanted to go back to the American zone and settle somewhere in the West.

'America or Australia. As far away as I can get from this god-forsaken place.'

As he had told me everything so quickly I was not sure whether to believe him, but I was happy to have company and so I told him I had been trying to cross the border for the past few days but that I kept on running into Soviet patrols.

'And they let you go?' he asked in bewilderment.

'Yes. I tell them a story about being lost – it's worked so far.'

I suggested that we team up until we got to the other side. With his fluent German, my Russian and his ID card as a Displaced Person we might stand a chance if they stopped us again. He reckoned that he knew where we were and where we could cross over easily. We shook hands on it and I felt relieved and full of confidence to be with someone who knew where he was going. In a couple of hours we could be free.

In the late afternoon he announced that he had found the path he had been looking for and that it would lead us down through the valley to safety.

'Follow me,' he said as I trotted along behind, no longer concentrating too intently, excited that the quest was nearly over. An hour later we walked straight into a Soviet patrol – three men and a corporal guarding the route over to the other side. It was no good running for it, there was nowhere to hide, but his ID card did the trick this time and I did my best to mutter just a few words of Russian to tell them we wanted to go to Poland.

'American zone, slave labour, we go home,' I said.

The corporal thought this was very funny and made a joke to his men about Poles being all brawn and no brain.

'You're all the same. Not enough grey matter! It's that way,' he said, pointing in the direction we had come. I did not mind him thinking we were stupid. The joke was on him, if only he had known it.

My confidence in my new friend had waned by the following morning because we had made no progress, but we stuck together and, after making a detour to please the last patrol, we found a German who pointed to a forest on the other side of the hill, saying that was where we needed to go. We followed his advice and proceeded with the greatest care for a mile or two, creeping up the wooded hillside away from the pathway through the trees. Then I noticed a clearing and, relieved to be out of the brambles, dropped my guard as I stepped into it.

'Halt! Who goes there?' shouted a voice.

We had almost reached the border and had run into yet another Soviet patrol, this time about half a dozen men with a staff sergeant. The sergeant had an odd expression and even odder attire, as he wore a yellow scarf round his neck, a battered trilby on his head and a rather fashionable, if worn, civilian coat over his uniform. A pair of shiny leather gloves peeped out of his coat pocket.

He asked us for our papers and we told him our story in Polish. He looked unimpressed and noted my Red Army boots, my lack of ID and the fact that I had absolutely nothing American or western on me. He was not as stupid as the corporal on the previous patrol.

'Well then, boys,' he said. 'You know you've broken the law and you know what the punishment is for breaking the law.'

I began to fear the worst, as he took off his coat and handed it with his scarf and hat to a subordinate, then rolled up his sleeves and slowly peeled on his leather gloves. With each movement he made grand theatrical gestures, as if performing for an audience.

'I'm going to teach them a lesson they won't forget in a hurry,' he said to the soldier holding his coat. 'Come here,' he said, beckoning to my companion. He rubbed his hands together and put up his fists. His method of punishment seemed to be to have a boxing match with us.

'No, no, don't hit me,' my new friend cried as the sergeant aimed a right hook at his chin. He went down on the ground after the first blow and started to beg for mercy. The sergeant told him to get up and gave him a couple more punches before he fell again, all the while pleading with him to stop and saying that he did not know he had done anything wrong. I felt slightly ashamed at his lack of courage and was determined to put up more resistance when my turn came, as it surely would. He punched me first in the stomach and then in the face, but neither blow seemed to hurt me. For a moment I thought I must have become impervious to pain and it took me a few seconds to realise that he was pretending to fight. I pretended to feel pain when the next punch landed on my chin.

'Let that be a lesson to the pair of you not to break the law in future. If I catch you again you won't be able to walk when I've finished with you. When I'm in command nobody escapes lightly.'

He put his hat and coat back on and pointed to a path leading through the woods.

'Carry on along that path for a mile and a half and you'll

come to Soviet troops who'll put you on a train to go home. If I catch you again, it'll be Siberia for the pair of you!'

We had no time to notice which direction he had sent us and followed his instructions without arguing. My friend was still trembling, as I was trying to keep up with him and work out for myself what had happened to us.

'He didn't hurt you,' I told him.

'Only because I begged him not to hurt me, that's why.'

'I didn't beg and he didn't hurt me,' I said.

I could not understand how somebody who claimed he had fought in the Wehrmacht could be afraid of a few punches.

We did not have to go as far as the eccentric sergeant had said before we came to a barn in a clearing where we could hear loud singing and the sounds of tables being banged with fists. We paused and it became obvious that there were soldiers inside having a raucous party. Russian and American soldiers were drinking together, we were told later. Not far beyond stood an American sergeant next to another man in uniform who turned out to be his German interpreter. After we had crept past the barn and approached the two of them to ask where we were, he made a sweeping gesture with his arm.

'This is the American zone.'

The American sergeant put his finger to his mouth and whispered 'Ssh' when his interpreter told him what we wanted. They walked a few yards with us before directing us to the road leading to Hof. The sergeant saluted and wished us luck as we said goodbye.

11

The End of the Free Poles

The two of us landed in a small transit camp in Hof, a small town in northern Bavaria on the new border between the Soviet and American zones. From there the Americans quickly transferred us to another camp, reserved in the main for Polish ex-combatants, at Langwasser near Nuremberg. Most of the Poles there were roughly my age, between seventeen and thirty, and all were men, the majority survivors of the Warsaw Uprising, now released from German captivity by the Allied victory. In addition, there were a few Yugoslavs and some Ukrainians, Latvians and Lithuanians, who, if they spoke enough Polish, attempted to claim Polish citizenship. All were seeking a future in the West. This is how many former SS troops and Nazi collaborators escaped, although the Allies returned nationals of the pre-war Soviet Union, such as Vlasov's men, to Stalin. Thankfully my own status was not open to doubt. I counted automatically as an ex-combatant because of my time with the partisans and the new Polish Air Force.

The options open to us were emigration to the USA, which took up to a year to arrange, or a transfer to the Free Polish Corps in Italy, which still formed part of the British Eighth Army under arms on the northern Adriatic coast. Some of the Warsaw Boys were drafted into Polish companies sent to guard the war criminals standing trial in Nuremberg. Had I gone with them, I might well have ended up in the United States as a GI.

I was still in Langwasser when the Americans dropped the

first atomic bombs on Hiroshima and Nagasaki. The whole camp cheered when the news came through, almost as loudly as we had cheered in Zamosc when Schlomin had announced the liberation of Warsaw in January that year. For us, the bombing signified one thing: that the West now had the military power to get Stalin to withdraw from Poland. Western military superiority was now beyond dispute. We felt that Churchill and Roosevelt had betrayed Poland by agreeing to the division of post-war Europe and that another war was infinitely preferable to the Soviet occupation of our country. Unfortunately, Polish and Western interests did not coincide. For the West, the war was now won and Europe was liberated, but Poland would not be truly free for more than forty years.

At the end of August I joined a queue to be screened for Italy and a week later I found myself sitting on a beach near Ancona with the Polish contingent of the Eighth Army. I joined a tank regiment in the Second Warsaw Mechanised Armour Division and soon commanded my own tank. In total the Free Poles had 300,000 men under arms in Italy by early 1946. My new life had its compensations. We picked ripe figs and peaches at the road-side and slept a stone's throw from the sea. The longer I stayed here, the more a feeling of relaxed well-being began to over-come my memories of beatings and hunger. I tasted a state of happiness for the first time in my adult life. We had meat with every meal, second helpings of every course, as much tea, coffee and cocoa as we could drink, and, of course, gallons of thick red wine, which was more readily available than fresh water. We were paid too. Yet it was during this period that guilt started to trouble me, however hard I tried not to think about all the things I had seen and done.

The origins of my comrades were diverse, but, generally speaking, we fell into three distinct categories. Perhaps a third had seen action in the North African and Italian campaigns, having for the most part been captured by the Soviets in 1939 and then released by Stalin in 1941 once the Soviet Union joined the war against Germany. These hardened veterans of the pre-war Polish army had not seen their native soil for more than six years. Another third were the Warsaw Boys who had survived the Uprising. They tended to be young and cocky. The last category were the traitors who had joined the Wehrmacht only to claim Polish nationality when the Allies overran their units. It was impossible to tell how many of these had fought voluntarily for the Germans and how many had been coerced. No one could check on each individual's history or establish his prior beliefs and allegiances. Even nationality could not always be proved conclusively, since an inability to speak Polish fluently did not necessarily mean that a man was not Polish by origin. All that could be said with any certainty was that the tables had now been turned: if it had previously been to some people's advantage to play up their German connections, the reverse was now the case. Naturally enough, there were tensions.

With my NKVD background I was soon asked to become involved in intelligence work, reporting on the political reliability of the troops. Radio Moscow was already making appeals for soldiers in the Polish Corps to desert, claiming that our current ranks and promotion prospects were guaranteed in the new Polish armed forces and stressing the opportunities in the new western territories which had been ceded by Germany. All this could sound very attractive, especially to the veterans who had not seen their homes for such a long time. The Italian Communist Party soon offered the equivalent of $100 for a deserting soldier's paybook. A few took up the offer and went back to Poland.

There was nothing, however, for me to report. The only Pole in the regiment who professed his preference for the Soviet Union did so with such vociferous insistence that he spent most of his time in the lock-up. No one else seemed inclined to agitate on Stalin's behalf. After all, the pre-war veterans had spent two years in his prison camps, while the Warsaw Boys were as staunchly anti-Bolshevik as they were anti-Nazi after their unique experience of fraternal co-operation. The only people who aroused my suspicions were the ex-Wehrmacht contingent. And so, as Stalinists seemed to be so thin on the ground, I decided to track down former Nazis.

I became suspicious of one man who eventually showed me a long burn scar underneath his right armpit, which had replaced the distinctive SS tattoo specifying his blood group. Burning was the only way of getting rid of the incriminating mark. By pretending I still admired Hitler myself, I coaxed him into telling me about the secret network in Italy which could help men like him out of their temporary difficulties. He said that the Vatican would arrange everything and get us both on a boat to Buenos Aires, but when I reported back to my superior officer he was quite uninterested in the case and told me to concentrate on Communist infiltrators. Once again, I felt betrayed.

At Easter 1946 the Communist government in Warsaw launched a major propaganda campaign against our continued presence in Italy, saying that the Free Polish Corps evidently had aggressive intentions, as otherwise it would disband rather than expand its numbers. Stalin complained to the British Prime Minister and influential elements within the British government agreed with the Soviets. This move led to the formation of the Polish Resettlement Corps or PRC, the purpose of which was to integrate demobilised combatants into civilian life somewhere in the West rather than in Communist Poland. In order to join, each individual signed a slip of paper, which, as Radio Moscow reminded us, entailed the renunciation of Polish citizenship. Until that signature was given, we still had the right to return to the new Poland.

Before signing I joined a section which travelled to Naples to board a boat to Liverpool and from there to a base a few miles outside Edinburgh. Here we led a secluded life, cut off from the local population, knowing too that the arrangement was temporary. In August General Anders, Commander in Chief of the Free Polish Forces, paid a visit to persuade us to sign up for the PRC. He arrived without fanfare and spoke without ceremony. Nevertheless his views were clouded in my opinion by his obsessive hatred of the Soviet Union, as he had been wounded by the Bolsheviks in 1920 and again in 1939. He gave a well-rehearsed speech in which he repeated, like a mantra, that 'united we stand, divided we fall', and implored us to sign the PRC document but remain within calling distance of the Government in Exile.

'I am not here to give orders or words of command. What I have are words of friendly advice from an old soldier to his fellow soldiers. Very shortly you will be discarding your uniforms and emigrating to the four corners of the earth. All I request is that you concentrate in countries where you can remain in touch and return to arms when need be.

'We have been let down by the Western governments,' he continued. 'The agreements made between us and them have been broken, but we must take heart from the fact that they have the weapons to secure a Soviet withdrawal from Polish territory. In the mean time we must understand that they are protecting their own interests. The West will not go to war for Poland, but as sure as I am standing here in front of you, Stalin will not forget his ambition of dominating the world and spreading the evil dogma of Communism. I have met Stalin and we have all seen what he is capable of doing. Only the date of the next war remains to be determined – it could start next week, next month, next year or in five years' time. We have to be ready when the time comes, for strike he will.'

Anders stayed in London, where he died in 1970. I saw him once more, twenty years later, when we had dinner together at the Polish Club in Kensington. He made no mention whatsoever of Polish freedom; he seemed much more interested in my companion's attractive wife.

After Anders' departure we transferred to Berwick-on-Tweed where we signed the PRC document and gradually began to disperse. We were given brochures about countries from all corners of the globe and shown letters of introduction from Polish college girls, particularly from New Zealand and Australia, looking for friendship and marriage. Anders had been disappointed that two divisions of Polish Desert Rats had taken the boat to Australia and New Zealand. There had been nothing he or the High Command could do to prevent them.

I could have applied to work in the coal mines in Britain, as there was a chronic shortage of miners despite relatively high wages, but the prospect of working underground did not appeal to me. Others wanted to join the British Army, the Merchant Navy or the French Foreign Legion. My first move was to apply for the RAF, as I had never given up my ambition to become a pilot. Unfortunately, I was told that I would have to do two years with the ground staff before I would have a chance of flying. In the end roughly a third of the men decided to go back home to Poland and another third left the UK to settle in other countries, mainly North America. In the end I joined a company of Poles sent to work with the Northumberland Fusiliers in Newcastle where I worked as a military policeman and interpreter, as my English was already better than most of my comrades'. In November 1947 I received confirmation that I could join the British Merchant Navy.

So began my new life in a new country. I was twenty-one years old.

Afterword

This book was written over two summers. Waldemar and I had met shortly after I had moved from Oxford, fresh from completing a doctorate on the works of the German-Polish novelist, Günter Grass, to a run-down part of East London where we found ourselves neighbours. I was briefly unemployed, at a loose end, and became fascinated when he started to tell me his tale.

When we began, I expected a fairly familiar story of survival in Nazi-occupied Poland and a notorious death camp. I felt that I knew what was coming and did not question my assumption that the camp experience would form the emotional core of the book – in the end, Majdanek takes up a mere ten per cent of the text and, dreadful though his time there obviously was, it by no means looms largest in his memory of horror.

Over five or six weeks that first summer, say 80 hours in all, since we met four afternoons a week for up to four hours at a stretch, we dealt with the material that would eventually feed into Chapter One. Progress was so slow because he spent days on end describing his childhood, his maternal grandparents, his schooling and his boyish antics in Kremenets, little of which has found its way into our final text. What began to puzzle and, increasingly, to irritate me was the way he emphasised his own acts of kindness to Ukrainian schoolchildren, which – he insisted – complemented official Polish benevolence towards the majority population in these eastern territories, which had become part of Poland in the aftermath of 1918. The frequency and scale of his acts of generosity bordered on the incredible.

For instance, he gave away his best mittens to a freezing class-mate in the sure knowledge he would receive a beating from his fierce mother when she found out, but did not regret his deed even once she had punished him. But when we got to the material which makes up Chapters Four and Five of this book, I began to understand what he had been saying and why. He wanted me to know that Poles and Ukrainians had been friends and that the violence unleashed on the Poles by their erstwhile neighbours was inexplicable to someone of his background. Perhaps he assumed I had some knowledge of this inferno, but my ignorance of it was total, which meant I was quite unprepared for it when it came.

In a statement reproduced in the Chronology at the end of this book, President Kravchuk of the Ukraine acknowledges that 500,000 Poles lost their lives to 'Ukrainian chauvinists' during the war. This figure, if it is accurate, must include those killed during the great population exchange after the German withdrawal, but does not take account of Ukrainians killed by Poles. The scale of this slaughter becomes apparent when one remembers that British casualties – military, Merchant Navy and civilian – in the Second World War totalled some 355,000. While it is always a treacherous business trying to establish casualty figures in this part of Europe, tens if not hundreds of thousands certainly did perish. Yet the whole episode is as good as unknown in the West. Part of the reason must be that the western Allies played no role in this theatre of war. While British SOE officers were dropped by parachute to fight with the partisans in Yugoslavia, and their memoirs record the struggle between Serbs and Croats, there exists no such western testimony covering the very similar conflict between Poles and Ukrainians. After 1945 neither Warsaw nor Moscow had any interest in keeping the story alive, and no one dreamed that Kiev would one day become the capital of an independent Ukraine. Waldemar was astonished when a relative sent him a biography of his CO in the Peasants' Battalions which made no mention of the massacres and instead concentrated on the heroic role the Resistance played fighting the Nazis. The Polish-

Ukrainian slaughter is barely mentioned in standard histories of the region: ours is the first book published in the UK to devote more than a sketchy paragraph to it.

There are gaps in Waldemar's knowledge, of course, and, it goes without saying, bias in his account, which I have not eradicated. He was unaware, despite the precision he brings to the description of the camp layout at Majdanek, that there had been gas chambers there, disputing that information when I first drew his attention to it. The gas chambers had ceased to function by the time he arrived in April 1944, by which time the other extermination camps of Operation Reinhard, Sobibor, Treblinka and Belzec, had been dismantled. He was also aghast that Belzec, a small village to the south of Lublin, synonymous for the rest of the world with genocide, had provided the site of an extermination camp at all. When he saw this written down he began singing a strange song with the name Belzec in the refrain, which his grandfather had sung to him when he was a boy. He tried to dispute the truth of published accounts that hundreds of thousands of Jews had been gassed at a site next to this little village by telling me how often his grandfather had visited the village in the long-gone, pre-war days. He wanted me to understand that he knew about Belzec; that was the point of the song, it was an innocent place and he would have known had there been a camp there. But he had not.

I assumed at the beginning, and I believe Waldemar assumed I assumed, that his views would be anti-Semitic, simply because I thought at the time that most Poles, like most East Europeans, still clung to anti-Semitism. When he began with recollections of his grandfather's Jewish friends, stressing how cordial and warm-hearted everything had been between them, how welcoming his grandfather's household had been to Jewish tradesmen, I felt sure that something was on his conscience or that he was set to excuse deeds by his compatriots. Whatever my suspicions at the outset, nothing ever came to the surface in this respect because there is nothing buried there. The three million Polish Jews murdered by the Nazis barely feature in his memoir because, with the exception of the Jewish children shot in the cemetery in Hrubieszow, his path barely crossed theirs. After the war in London Waldemar mixed with Jewish refugees from Eastern Europe. They spoke the same languages as he did and liked the same sorts of food. With his long beard, black hat and dark overcoat, his wife's one-time employer was probably not the only person to mistake him for a rabbi.

Because he has carried his whole story with him for so long, and despite attempting to forget it for many years, he feels sure both of minute details and of his overview of the wider picture. He has thought over and over again about distances, sequences, measurements, numbers, even dates, turning them over and over in his mind and he now insists that everything he recalls is absolutely accurate. It often seemed to me that he took refuge from the emotional pain of remembering by concentrating on these details, always telling me how far it was between two points, two people or two buildings, correcting himself and revising his estimate until he was happy that it was right. The leitmotif of the tale of his survival in Laskuv had nothing to do with his fear, his proximity to death, or his desperation and amazing luck. The point he came back to again and again was whether the unlucky Polish platoon that was surprised that dawn contained 47 or 49 men. Two of them survived; 45 or 47 died. Somehow, if he could be sure of the numbers, the story would be complete. As far as he is concerned, that is probably the biggest weakness in this entire book.

In the second summer, after meeting every fortnight when I was back home from a new lecturing job in the North of England, we covered the remaining two-thirds of the material. Majdanek took no more than three days: he had prepared himself in advance. I had gained his trust, he was ready with what he wanted to say and the story was by and large worked out in his mind. It goes without saying that his story continued to astonish me – the swiftness of the transition to the post-war settlement under the Red Army in Poland, for instance. The way Waldemar goes directly from concentration camp to the Red Air Force is a telling metaphor for his country's fate. His decision to desert and join the Free Poles in their hopeless guerrilla

Afterword

campaign against the new occupiers illustrates, again, the way loyalties were tested and how the Poles were destined to lose out. This was all unknown history to me. Even his walk west to Germany, the land of his persecutors, and the time he subsequently spent in Italy brought to the surface facts and themes which have received little attention.

Waldemar's life afterwards is interesting primarily because of the way in which it was shaped by his past. After a decade in the Merchant Navy, where he advanced from stoker to third engineer, he never really settled down to a steady job in London, working in factories, as a mini-cab driver or a vacuum-cleaner salesman. While he often worked with émigré Jews from his part of the world, he was bankrupted by a Polish-American business partner when he set up his own firm to export meat to his compatriots in the early 1980s. His health has been poor since then.

I have re-arranged and re-structured his tale, re-phrased much of it, ironed out inconsistencies or made him do so and made him check the chronology and fill the few gaps left in his narrative, but that was largely editorial work. Our book is his monument, a monument to his survival, which is why he wanted to dedicate it to those who did not survive.

Julian Preece

Chronology
of Polish History, 1918–1945

1914–18

As their historic territory has been divided between Russia, Austria-Hungary and Germany since the partitions of the late eighteenth century, Poles fight on both sides in the First World War. Some 450,000 Polish soldiers lose their lives. Poland becomes a battlefield for the duration of the war, as German and Austro-Hungarian troops march from the west and south to do battle with the Russians from the east.

1918

As the three partitioning powers all collapse, Poland becomes free. Its border with Germany is decided by the Treaty of Versailles in spring 1919; those in the east with the newly created state of Lithuania and the Soviet Union by a combination of negotiation and military action in the Russo-Polish War of 1918–1921.

In order to guard against a resurgent Russia, Marshal Pilsudski initially favours a Commonwealth of Three Nations, forged principally from three provinces of the disintegrating Tsarist empire, Poland itself, Lithuania (Poland's historic partner) and the Ukraine, where hopes for independence flicker briefly under Semyon Petlura. Disputes over Pilsudski's home town of Vilnius, capital of today's Lithuania which ultimately fell to Poland in 1920, and Lwow, scene of heavy fighting between the

Polish and Ukrainian population, make co-operation between Poles and Ukrainians fraught. A West Ukrainian People's Republic lasts from November 1918 to July 1919.

1920

The post-war Polish state contains many non-Poles: Germans (2.5 per cent) and Ukrainians (17 per cent), as well as a large unassimilated Jewish population (10 per cent). More than 2 million Poles are still left outside Poland, whose territories in the Middle Ages and early modern period had extended much further eastward.

The seeds for future ethnic conflict have been sown, as another chronicler of the massacres explains:

Meanwhile, shortly after gaining military control over Western Ukraine in 1919, and in violation of the Versailles Treaty on the treatment of minorities, the Polish government began to take a series of retaliatory measures against the Ukrainians who had fought against them in the recent Polish-Ukrainian (1918–19) war. Among these measures was the arrest and deportation of several thousand Ukrainians, as well as the promulgation of policies antithetic to Ukrainian sociopolitical life. This in turn prompted Ukrainian strikes, boycotts, demonstrations and isolated acts of terror, assassinations, bombings, and sabotage [...] during the 1920s against Polish authority.
(Tadeusz Piotrowski, *Vengeance of the Swallows*, p.39)

1923

The *Bierkellerputsch* in Munich led by the little-known Austrian war veteran, ex-corporal Adolf Hitler.

1930

A Ukrainian nationalist organisation begins a campaign of anti-government terrorism in the eastern areas of Poland. The authorities respond with what amount to anti-insurgency measures, including the burning of villages and the internment of Ukrainian activists.

In the Soviet Ukraine, millions are deported or starved to death in the 1930s during the collectivisation of agriculture which aims to eliminate the kulaks as a socio-economic group.

1932

Non-aggression pact signed between Poland and the Soviet Union.

1934

Poland signs a ten-year non-aggression pact with Hitler, since 30 January 1933 the German *Reichskanzler*.

The Polish Minister of the Interior is assassinated by Ukrainians. An agreement between the two sides then ensures an uneasy peace until the outbreak of war.

1938

March: German forces march into Vienna to enforce the so-called *Anschluss* of Austria.

October: Hitler is permitted by an agreement with Britain and France to dismantle the Czechoslovakian Republic, absorbing the German-populated Sudetenland into the Reich.

1939

March: Hitler annexes the rump of what was Czechoslovakia.

Britain promises to defend Polish independence in the event of a German attack.

Warsaw refuses to countenance an alliance with the Soviet Union for fear that, if Soviet troops take up positions on Polish soil, they will never withdraw.

23 August: The Molotov-Ribbentrop Pact between Nazi Germany and the Soviet Union, sworn ideological enemies, is announced to an astonished world. A secret protocol provides for the partition of Poland along the old Curzon Line following the Rivers Bug and San, which becomes the new Polish-Soviet border in 1945.

1 September: Germany invades Poland, putting the theory of Blitzkrieg into practice for the first time. The Poles fight fiercely, inflicting much heavier losses on the Germans than anyone, except the Poles themselves, had expected.

17 September: Soviet troops enter Poland from the east and occupy that part of the country assigned to them under the agreement with Germany. Of the 12 million inhabitants conquered by the Red Army, only about 5 million are ethnic Poles, most of the remainder Ukrainians. By June 1941, when Germany invades the Soviet Union, some 2 million Poles have been deported to Siberia or Kazakhstan, where as many as half perish. The Soviets take 200,000 Polish POWs and murder more than 25,000 officers, 4,000 of whom are buried in mass graves at Katyn, discovered there in April 1943:

The treatment of the Poles by the Soviet Union between 1939 and 1941 is still an unfamiliar story to foreigners [...] The true story emerged only in fragments during the post-war years, and was understandably overshadowed by the more spectacular and better-publicised savageries of the Nazi occupation of Poland and the rest of Europe. Yet in its brutality and the sheer scale of its cold-blooded attempt to obliterate the Polish nation physically and culturally, this 21-month Soviet occupation far outdid all the crimes committed against Poland during the century and a quarter of Russian occupation under the Tsars.
(Neal Ascherson, *The Struggles for Poland*, pp.94–5)

5 October: The last shots of the Polish campaign are fired. The Polish government escapes to represent the defeated country in exile, first in Paris, then London. General Sikorski is appointed Prime Minister.

The western parts of Poland are absorbed into the German Reich; central Poland comes under the control of the 'General Government' based in Lublin and headed by the notorious Hans Frank, hanged at Nuremberg for crimes against humanity. Polish culture is systematically extinguished, property confiscated and able-bodied men and women are sent to the Reich as forced labourers. Poles are stripped of all rights and declared an inferior race. Shootings and summary executions start immediately, intensifying in number and brutality as the war progresses.

The Polish Resistance begins immediately and takes many forms. Unlike in Western Europe, there is no systematic collaboration with the enemy. The Government in Exile seeks to organise the multitude of Resistance factions and individual combat units, many of which reflect political affiliations and splits from pre-war days, under the umbrella of the Home Army. The Peasants' Battalions, associated with the pre-war Peasants' Party, are the third largest grouping after the conservative Home Army and the left-leaning People's Army. The Home Army's strategy is to prepare for a general uprising once the Germans have come to their knees. Acts of sabotage generally result in savage reprisals which risk alienating sections of the civilian population.

1941

21 June: The German invasion of the Soviet Union, code-named Operation Barbarossa, begins. Western Ukrainians welcome the Germans as liberators; Latvians and Lithuanians also provide a source of willing recruits and many serve as concentration camps guards alongside Ukrainian volunteers:

Tens of thousands of Ukrainians enlisted in the local police and volunteered for the German security forces. The majority of these Ukrainians were former soldiers of the Red Army who had fallen into German captivity. Nazi Germany encouraged Ukrainian prisoners of war, as well as Lithuanians, Latvians, Estonians, and others, to join their ranks, and thousands responded to their call. Some of them did it to escape the horrible conditions in which Soviet prisoners of war were kept, others for nationalistic reasons, hoping to receive some kind of Ukrainian independence within the framework of a Nazi Europe as a reward for their services. Many joined the ranks of the Nazis for reasons of anti-Semitism, which was quite common among the Ukrainians and other East European nations, or for economic profit. Other Ukrainians who joined the German security forces were local people, most of them inhabitants of Polish West Ukraine. The Ukrainians served in special units of the German army, the SS, and the police.
(*Yitzhak Arad*, Belzec, Sobibor, Treblinka, p.20)

30 July: Under pressure from the British, and in the face of opposition from his colleagues, Sikorski signs a Polish-Soviet agreement in London.

Polish soldiers captured in 1939 by the Soviets are now encouraged to gather from the farthest flung points in Siberia to form an army under the authority of the Government in Exile. General Wladyslaw Anders is put in command. After two years in prison in Moscow, he is understandably anti-Soviet and wants to fight the Germans with the western Allies. Sikorski wants the forces to stay in the Soviet Union and to join the fighting on the Eastern Front, thus maintaining some leverage over Stalin and ensuring that Polish troops will be among the liberators of Poland. In August 1942 some 115,000 Polish soldiers, who had continued to suffer severe deprivation after regrouping, begin to arrive in British-controlled Iran. This is part of the army which Waldemar joined in Italy in the summer of 1945.

December: The Germans are halted at the gates of Moscow and Leningrad.

One German murder squad was set to work in Jozefow, where Waldemar was captured in April 1944 after stumbling out of the Puszcza Solska. Christopher Browning gives a gruesome account in a pioneering book:

As darkness approached at the end of a long summer day and the murderous task was still not finished, the shooting became even less organised and more hectic. The forest was so full of dead bodies that it was difficult to find places to make the Jews lie down. When darkness finally fell about 9.00 p.m. – some seventeen hours after the Reserve Police Battalion 101 had first arrived on the outskirts of Jozefow – and the last Jews had been killed, the men returned to the marketplace and prepared to depart for Bilgoraj. No plans had been made for the burial of the bodies and the dead Jews were simply left lying in the woods.

(Christopher Browning, *Ordinary Men*, pp.68–9)

1942

October: The siege of Stalingrad begins. Hitler refuses to allow the German commander to retreat, thus sealing the fate of 200,000 men of the German Sixth Army. Stalingrad falls the following February, the turning point of the war.

1943

13 April: German radio announces the discovery of mass graves at Katyn containing the bodies of Polish officers. Even though the news is treated with suspicion, as it serves Nazi purposes to drive a wedge between the Soviets and the Poles, it appears more and more probable that the officers were murdered by Soviet forces in the spring of 1940.

May: Stalin sets up a pro-Soviet Polish army under the command of Zygmunt Berling, made up of Polish soldiers who were unable to join Anders and Soviet citizens of Polish descent.

Poles thus fight with the Soviet forces which liberate the country in 1944-45. Waldemar encountered some of these men in the so-called Red Polish Air Force.

November–December: Conference of the 'Big Three' (Stalin, Roosevelt and Churchill) in Teheran where it is agreed to shift both the western and eastern borders of Poland some 200 miles westwards. The Government in Exile, now led by Mikoljaicek after Sikorski's death, never accepts this change.

1944

January: The Red Army crosses the pre-war eastern Polish border.

May: Polish soldiers under General Anders fight courageously with the Allies in the Italian campaign, most famously breaking the siege of Monte Cassino.

22 July: The Soviet-backed Polish Committee of National Liberation issues its July Manifesto and moves to Lublin in Soviet-liberated Poland when it is recognised by Moscow as the legitimate authority in Poland.

25 July: Soviet forces under the command of Marshall Rokossowsky reach the outskirts of Warsaw.

1 August to 2 October: Warsaw Uprising. The Soviets refuse to come to the Poles' aid, preferring to let the Germans deal with the nationalist Home Army. There are approximately 200,000 Polish casualties. On Hitler's express orders, Warsaw is razed to the ground by the retreating Germans.

1945

17 January: Troops from the Berling Army finally enter Warsaw. The whole of the reconstituted country comes under Soviet

control. Poland has lost a higher percentage of its population than any other pre-war state:

As a result of almost six years of war, Poland lost 6,028,000 of its citizens, or 22 per cent of its total population, the highest ratio of losses to population of any country in Europe. About 50 per cent of these victims were Polish Christians and 50 percent were Polish Jews. Approximately 5,384,000, or 89.9 per cent, of Polish war losses (Jews and Gentiles), were the victims of prisons, death camps, raids, executions, annihilation of ghettos, epidemics, starvation, excessive work and ill treatment.
(Richard C. Lukas, *The Forgotten Holocaust*, pp.38–9)

The war in Europe that ends on 8 May 1945 continues in Poland for up to two more years. While the Home Army disarms and demobilises in July, independent units carry on fighting, particularly in the south-east of the country:

The Terror launched by the Soviets was answered in kind. Village mayors, local electoral officers and police agents installed by the NKVD were murdered, or harassed and subjected to reprisals. Entire districts, especially in the Carpathians, fell into the hands of bandit kings, like the terrible 'Kapitan Ogien' (Captain Fire) of Zakopane. From the Soviet point of view, these developments proved most convenient, providing the best possible excuse for perpetuating their hold on the security services.
(Norman Davies, *God's Playground*, Vol.2, p.560)

The new state is ethnically and religiously the most homogeneous in Polish history: most Germans are expelled to the west, and those who stay do so largely surreptitiously and assimilate; Ukrainians west of the Bug are exchanged for Poles living east of the river; in turn, Poles from these eastern provinces settle in the towns and villages vacated by the Germans. This is one of the greatest population shifts in European history.

Postscript

1989–92

To surprise and relief in Poland and the Ukraine, the wounds of conflict do not re-open with the dismantling of the USSR and the collapse of the Soviet bloc. Indeed, during a visit to Warsaw in May 1992, Leonid Kravchuk, the first president of independent Ukraine, officially acknowledges and apologises for the Ukrainian attacks on Polish villages:

We do not conceal and do not keep silent. During the Second World War Ukrainian chauvinists killed about half a million Polish people in the eastern regions of pre-September Poland. Likewise, for a number of years after the war Polish villages burned and people perished. Ukrainian chauvinism is an abscess on the healthy body of the Ukrainian nation, a pang of our conscience in respect to the Polish nation.
(Quoted by Tadeusz Piotrowski, *The Vengeance of the Swallows*, p.91)

But the spirit of reconciliation did not reign everywhere in Europe. Waldemar's story proved to be still alive in the mid-1990s as the war in Bosnia reached new heights. The actions of Bosnian Serbs against Muslim civilians were reported in the daily bulletins as he told the story of the Ukrainian massacres. These atrocities seemed to be a re-run of the ethnic massacres that had occurred fifty years earlier in an adjacent part of Eastern Europe. After seeing on television the charred remains of victims dragged from dug-outs in their gardens, Waldemar remembered how he had come across similar scenes. Whole families of Poles or Ukrainians tried to save themselves by hiding in holes they dug themselves, covering the entrances to these makeshift shelters with branches and undergrowth. They hoped that their attackers would assume that they had fled and would burn down their houses before moving off in pursuit. That way they lost their homes but saved themselves. But the attackers grew wise to this tactic, sought out the dug-outs by trampling through the gardens and hurled in a hand-grenade or riddle the huddled victims with bullets. What happened then, in 1944 in the county of Lublin, was happening now again in ex-Yugoslavia: the past was not past after all.

Select Bibliography

Lt.-General W. Anders, *An Army in Exile: The Story of the Second Polish Corps* (Macmillan: London, 1949).

Catherine Andreyev, *Vlasov and the Russian Liberation Movement: Soviet Reality and Emigré Theories* (Cambridge University Press: Cambridge, 1987) gives the background to the Kalmuk renegades.

Yitzhak Arad, *Belzec, Sobibor, Treblinka: The Operation Reinhard Death Camps* (Indiana University Press: Bloomington, 1987).

Neal Ascherson, *The Struggles for Poland* (Pan Books: London, 1988).

Christopher Browning, *Ordinary Men: Reserve Police Battalion 101 and the Final Solution in Poland* (HarperCollins: New York, 1992).

Norman Davies, *God's Playground: A History of Poland* (Oxford University Press: Oxford, 1981).

Alfred Döblin, *Journey to Poland,* (Tauris: London, 1991), describes the ethnic tensions in the region in the immediate aftermath of the First World War.

Primo Levi, *If Not Now, When?* (Abacus: London, 1987), the best fictional account available in English of a group of partisans in Poland and the Ukraine.

Richard C. Lukas, *The Forgotten Holocaust: The Poles under German Occupation 1939–1944* (University Press of Kentucky: Lexington, 1986).

Tadeusz Piotrowski, *Vengeance of the Swallows: Memoirs of a Polish Family's Ordeal* (McFarland: North Carolina, 1995) covers the massacres which took place east of the Bug.

Orest Subtelny, *Ukraine: A History* (University of Toronto Press: Toronto, 1988).

Acknowledgements

Both Waldemar and I are grateful to members of our families for their practical and emotional support: to Ellen for her good humour and limitless supplies of tea, to Pippa, who thought up the title, Christine for her unswerving faith, and to Matthew, Anthony, Marianne and Gabriel, who often wondered what was going on. My father, who died in April 1997 and had his own memories of a very different sort of war in South Wales, would have been proud to see this book in print. He was its first critical reader. My colleague Martin Kane and friend Greg Bond gave useful advice. Sheila Holness proved indefatigable with her assistance.

I profited too from the resources of the incomparable Wiener Library for Contemporary History and the Polish Institute and Sikorksi Museum in London.

Julian Preece